Money Assassins

Money Assassins

*How they stole your financial freedom
and how you can get it back*

Chad Viminitz

Library and Archives Canada Cataloguing in Publication

Viminitz, Chad, 1975-
Money assassins : how they stole your financial freedom and how you can get it back / Chad Viminitz.

ISBN 978-1-897178-82-9

1. Finance, Personal. 2. Saving and investment. 3. Debt. I. Title.

HG179.V55 2009   332.024   C2009-904551-6

The publisher gratefully acknowledges the support of the Department of Canadian Heritage through the Book Publishing Industry Development Program.

Printed and bound in Canada

Insomniac Press
520 Princess Ave., London, Ontario, Canada, N6B 2B8
www.insomniacpress.com

For my daughter Olivia in hopes of a more just and healthy world.

Acknowledgements

There may be one name on the front cover, but this book has not been a solo project.

I would like to thank family, friends, and colleagues for listening and encouraging me in what must have felt like a never ending process. Special thanks to RTR Advisory Group for your support and patience. Scott your eye for style is always appreciated. Bruce Campbell, if it was not for our hours of conversation and debate this book would not be here. To my colleagues, I am grateful for the skills and opportunities you have provided me throughout my career. To everyone who combed through drafts of the manuscript your feedback was invaluable. Mark Anielski, thank you for being generous with your time and advice.

To those who helped me write and edit the manuscript, I am forever indebted. Thank you to Ken Bond for taking on what, at times seemed like a daunting task, of structuring the book into a cohesive format and taking time away from your amazing family. Matthew Mitchell you are wise beyond your years, you are not only family, but a great friend; your influence is felt throughout these pages.

At Insomniac Press, I owe thanks to Mike O'Connor for seeing the importance of having my message published. To Gillian Urbankiewicz for your hours of editing and attention to detail, you made the editing process easy. To Curtis Rostad at Trafick for implementing the website. My agent Brian Wood, I am appreciative of the time you gave to the book. The amazing and talented team at Outright Communications, Rachel, Crystal, and Tanya, your commitment to the project has been a source of encouragement and success.

Without the cast of characters that make up my family, I would not be the person I am today. Thank you to my mom who gave me the gift to chase dreams, to be a good listener, and to help others. To my dad who gave me the love of reading, the love of the outdoors and whose help on the book is cherished. To my sister who reminds me to see the positive. To my in-laws Mary Anne and Ian Mitchell, thank you for your help on the home front allowing me the necessary time to get this project completed. To my cousin Sasha, thank you for the countless conversations around the dinner table and encouragement to take a writing class.

Last but certainly not least, I owe the most to my wife Becci. I thank you for lending me your brilliant mind, keen eye, amazing gift of writing and for the hours of editing, even while pregnant. Your brutal honesty made this a better book. We have created a special, unique, and privileged life together and I love you for that. You and Olivia matter most. I wrote this book to make our lives and the lives of our children and grandchildren stronger, healthier, and more just. I hope I have succeeded.

Table of Contents

Introduction

Who Are the Money Assassins?

If a team of archeologists began digging below North America's landscape, they would find remnants of past civilizations that prioritized saving over spending, cash over debt, delayed gratification over instant gratification, and a "waste not, want not" lifestyle, as opposed to the convenience of consumerism. Buried deep beneath today's current consumption-oriented, technologically-driven, debt-dependent culture is a lost art form that has the power to bring about a financial, social, and environmental revolution. It is only with the revitalization of the lost art of saving that this potential and explosive power can be realized. However, quietly operating under the radar since the 1970s, the "Money Assassins" have worked hard to destroy the art of saving, eroding the foundation of financial well-being, tarnishing pearls of financial wisdom, and making financial common sense a relic of the past. This assault on financial thought and behaviour has left many with record levels of debt and economically vulnerable as a result of historically low savings.

Since the 1970s, the evolution of consumer society, advancements in technology, and increasing access to debt have helped shape and mold the financial psyche of millions of North Americans. I call the collective but independent work of these three forces the "Money Assassins." My goal throughout the course of this book is to expose the Money Assassins for what they really are: opponents of our financial well-being. These forces have succeeded in assaulting our financial stability by covertly integrating themselves into the fabric of our everyday lives. As we will discover through the chapters of this book, it is only after gaining an understanding and awareness of the role that the Money Assassins play in our lives that we can begin to eliminate debt and create wealth.

There is a degree of irony in the fact that we have a national savings rate that hovers around 0 percent and record levels of personal debt despite living in the "information age" where we have more financial knowledge and advice at our fingertips than at any other time in history. Countless surveys reveal that people know they should save more, spend less, maximize their retirement savings, and cut up their credit cards. There is some truth to the old adage that "the road to hell is paved with good intentions"; many of us have good intentions, though we have been walking down this financial road for some time. What can explain our failure to choose the right financial path? Why are so many of us aimlessly following this path, even when we know danger lies ahead?

Reviving and mastering the art of saving begins with rediscovering our financial mindset, perspectives, and priorities. Many financial strategies and ideas work well in theory, but given the financial reality created by the Money Assassins, what works in theory appears to be failing individuals and families in their day-to-day financial realities. (1) Financially lost and desperately wanting to get back on track, many of us look for "silver bullet" solutions. While no such solutions exist, we often look to investment analyses, tax strategies, and spreadsheet projections to provide us with financial miracles. The result, however, generally leads to increased levels of frustration and financial disappointment. It is not that these strategies or ideas are inherently flawed, but rather that they fail to connect with our core values and beliefs. These band-aid solutions serve to only temporarily conceal our financial wounds instead of dealing with the underlying problem. In other words, no meaningful change occurs in our financial mindsets and lifestyles. Clearly, then, the challenge at hand is for us to understand and gain awareness of ourselves and our individual financial situations.

It is my hope that gaining this awareness and understanding of ourselves, and of the Money Assassins, will result in a life of financial well-being. The term *financial well-being* is open to much interpretation and will mean something different to each reader. To me it means having the financial ability to create the authentic life you truly desire. Financial ability is inclusive of both one's monetary and philosophical capabilities. To some this will mean early retirement, paying for their children's education, becoming debt free, buying recreational property, or having a million dollars. To others it will mean spending more time with family and friends, volunteering for worthy causes, enjoying hobbies, having time for reflection, or achieving peace of mind. I prefer the term *financial well-being* to *financial success* because it gives us permission to broaden the definition of what we are trying to achieve. It recognizes that conditions of happiness or prosperity can, of course, be material wealth, but it also gives consideration to what joy or delight can bring into our lives.

A Journey of Understanding

I got into the financial services industry because I wanted to help people. I believed that my clients, with a little guidance and advice, could significantly improve their financial well-being and achieve financial peace of mind and security. However, I soon realized that with North Americans spending more than they make, incurring record levels of personal debt, and having little to no savings, the issue was not so much about helping my clients with their financial plan, but instead about helping them find the money to commit to their plan. This realization occurred in 2001 while I was working in Vancouver as a product manager with one of Canada's largest financial organizations. I remember discussing the matter with Bruce Campbell, a colleague at the time, and a friend of mine. Bruce and I were puzzled by the following question: "Why can't people save?" We simply could not wrap our heads around why so many smart, well-intended, and hard-working people were struggling with their personal finances; something in the financial industry was awry, but we just couldn't quite put our finger on it.

Over the course of my career, I have had the privilege of living and working across Western Canada. This has provided me with the opportunity to discuss many financial questions with a wide variety of professionals. The question that most puzzled me was why people seemed to disregard well-established and sound financial principles, the most basic being "spend less than you make." In discussing the question with many of my colleagues, I was surprised to hear their answers. Their answers struck me as being overly simplistic, ill-informed, and insulting to the intelligence of many individuals. I simply could not believe that our poor financial habits were intrinsically linked to our lack of self-discipline, the poor choices that we made on a regular basis, and financial illiteracy. Unsatisfied with these answers, I set out to find out for myself what was driving the financial behaviour of countless individuals who, in many respects, should have had high levels of financial well-being and financial security. Finding answers to these questions has become a great passion of mine. The fruit of my investigations are found in the pages of this book.

In beginning my journey to understand how and why our financial perspectives and behaviour have changed so profoundly in recent years, I have come to appreciate the complexity of this question. While I was hoping to find clear and basic answers to the problem, I soon realized that my investigation would necessitate a holistic approach to addressing the multiple factors at work that shape our financial behaviour. Former Harvard Professor and author David Korten speaks to the need to address the complexities of such a question. According to Korten, "academia organizes intellectual inquiry into narrowly specialized disciplines. Consequently, we become accustomed to dealing with complex issues in fragmented bits and pieces. Yet we live in a complex world in which nearly every aspect of our lives is connected in some way with every other aspect." (2) It did not take me long to understand that financial planning and well-being were no different. My journey into understanding the root causes of financial behaviour has taken me many places that I would never have anticipated. My research into this book led me into such fields as philosophy, sociology, marketing, politics, and history, as I quickly realized that the answers I was looking for were to be found by examining combinations of these respective disciplines. Every time I came across new research, I realized that I did not fully understand the problems and challenges people were facing. To find the answers I was looking for, I would need to study society as a whole to understand the relationship between our social, political, and economic environments.

One of the most alarming things I learned from my research is that the financial habits of our society are perceived very differently by various professions. The more I researched and began writing, the angrier and more frustrated I became, especially at the so-called "experts," often economists, who continually preached that there is no need to worry about a negative national savings rate and record levels of personal debt. Economists tend to examine savings and debt at the national economic level. What this means is that consumer spending, which is considered to be one of the main drivers of a country's economic growth, is looked upon pretty favourably. Therefore, from the economist's perspective, as long as individuals and families are able to continue to spend and make debt payments, everything is okay. However, the reality "on the ground" for individuals and families is much gloomier: longer work days, longer commutes, less sleep, less family time, greater financial hardship, and anxiety over debt. While the "experts" were able to ignore this reality until the recent credit crisis, it became clear to me that there is an urgent need for a financial awakening on the part of society. In my opinion, the dominant financial buzzwords of our day—*consume*, *debt*, and *invest*—needed to be replaced with a vocabulary that included *thrift*, *frugality*, and *saving*. Although these words speak to a lost financial way of life, the adoption of these words into our collective vocabulary is an essential ingredient in the revitalization of our financial well-being. While the lost art of saving may be largely forgotten, this book will help revive it and provide a road map for us to get back on track to the road to financial success and well-being.

Beginning Your Journey

Most of us have been left on our own to survive the financial trappings of our current economy. For many years now, you may have had a gut feeling that something has not been right in your financial life but have been unable to pinpoint exactly what it is. It is a mystery why so many of us have done nothing to stop ourselves from the financial harms we see ahead and instead have continued to move onward. As a collective, we have underestimated the influence of the Money Assassins and their culminating effect on our financial lives. The Money Assassins have become commonplace and have formed the backdrop of our daily lives by creating an economic system that sets us up for failure. This is a conclusion many will find difficult to accept as we live in a society that blindly promotes the virtues of personal choice, independence, and freedom, yet underestimates the power of persuasion and the fear of social exclusion.

Being open to new ideas about finance and money is crucial if you hope to achieve financial well-being. When reading this book, I ask you to put your guard down and read with an open mind. This is not to suggest that I'm discouraging you from thinking critically or disagreeing with what you read—I encourage both—but you should be open to new ideas and perspectives in order for positive change to take shape. Think of the mind as a cup of tea. If your cup is full of your own ideas, and fresh tea is poured in to the cup, the tea will spill over. You must, therefore, empty some of the tea to make room for the new.

To get the most out of this book, you must journey to the root of your financial psyche, a journey that will undoubtedly be uncomfortable and unsettling at times. Financial anxiety is one of the largest causes of chronic stress in our lives. To overcome this anxiety, we need to address it head-on. Preparing ourselves for this journey requires a great deal of introspection, which is a challenging task for most people. You are going to need the courage to see the truth and to let go of the familiar and secure. A financial turnaround requires both courage and imagination. To lack courage is to accept conformity and, given the record levels of debt and low levels of savings, conforming to the financial reality of the millions of people in our society in troubled financial situations is clearly not a desirable option. We must summon and ignite the courage within us all so we may act in accordance with our true values and beliefs. It is only through concrete action that our financial lives will change and move in the direction of our true desires. The path to freedom, financial freedom in our case, is a road less travelled that necessitates great courage and a commitment to change.

In their book *Your Money or Your Life*, Joe Dominguez and Vicki Robin give their readers permission to feel no guilt or shame about their current financial situation. I would also encourage you to do the same. Regardless of the stage or time in your life that you pick up this book, there is hope to achieve financial well-being, as financial well-being is not a figure or a measure in years, but rather a mindset and lifestyle. I strongly believe that the financial position that many of us find ourselves in is a result of an economic system designed to promote consumption over financial well-being. With little financial guidance available to help us navigate these new and uncharted waters, it is no wonder that many of us are struggling to keep our heads above the water.

My hope is that you will gain an appreciation for the complex factors that help shape our spending habits and financial decisions. Because there are no easy answers, I would encourage you to read through all of the chapters in the order set out in the book, as each chapter builds on the discussions in preceding chapters. Throughout the book, you will be asked to do some financial calculations to give yourself a clearer picture of your finances. It is critical that you do them, as the results will pinpoint the most important areas in which you must first turn to address your financial situation. To help you with these calculations, a number of financial calculators have been set up at *www.moneyassassins.com*. After going through the book in its entirety, I would encourage you to return to specific chapters that are most important to your financial plan.

I sincerely hope that after reading *Money Assassins* you will feel inspired to share it with others. Having discovered this new financial plan, you will be able to help friends, family, and colleagues—all of the people that you care about—discover the secret to financial independence. This is a gift that can last a lifetime and influence generations to come. It is the action of others that is the greatest of persuasions; we must be the action and change that others see and admire. Don't keep this book a secret; there is a great deal of urgency in exposing the Money Assassins before they ruin more financial lives. There is no silver bullet to the financial challenges we face, but I hope you will find this book to be a valuable resource and a first step in reviving the lost art of saving.

Organization of the Book

This book is written in two parts. Part one consists of four chapters. These chapters are more descriptive in nature than those in the second part of the book and provide a commentary on economic changes since the 1970s. These chapters will serve to explain major developments in the construction of your financial belief system, and how certain factors have influenced your financial behaviour. Part two consists of five chapters but is much more prescriptive than the first part of the book. In these chapters, I will provide you with straightforward, proven, and effective financial and lifestyle advice that will serve to help you develop a financial plan that will result in less debt and help create more wealth.

The first chapter of this book, "The Great Forgetting," takes valuable lessons from the past and applies them to today. I will focus on the period of 1929–1939, the Great Depression, as this period heavily influenced the financial mindsets of successive generations. Barry Broadfoot, author of *Ten Lost Years*, has argued that the vast majority of people know nothing, or very little, about this period, even though it has influenced so much of our world today. (3) This is partly because so few books have been written about this period, especially financial planning books that might use the events of this period to illustrate some important financial lessons that can be learned from it. This chapter will examine how the generation that survived this period became the greatest savers in history, how their experiences during the Great Depression and World War II led to astute saving habits and cultural maxims such as "a penny saved is a penny earned." Furthermore, it will examine how, for millions of people, their experience during this period shook them to their core, making them seriously reflect on the values of their society and their own personal and financial values. As this chapter will show, the development of rigid financial behaviour and values helped create the strongest middle class in history. This generation of savers accumulated unprecedented levels of wealth without studying financial theory. They distrusted financial institutions, praised thriftiness and frugality, saved money under their mattresses, and equated debt with slavery. In reading through this chapter, I hope you will be able to gain important insights into the first steps of how to rebuild your financial belief structure, learn the value of financial empathy, and see the sharp contrast between the role government played in assisting individuals with their financial well-being in the past as compared with the present. I strongly believe that developing an awareness of our past is a critical first step to creating wealth and eliminating debt in the present.

In the second chapter, "Wealth, Happiness, and the First Assassin," we will examine some of the factors that have influenced the changes to our financial belief structure by looking at the evolving nature of our definitions of wealth and happiness. We will explore how the *perception* of wealth has taken over *actual* wealth as the main objective for many. We will also explore concepts such as relativism, social positioning, financial "waste," and challenge traditional measurements of economic progress. As indicated by the title of this chapter, we will also introduce the First Assassin: technology.

When I began writing *Money Assassins*, I never would have imagined that a chapter on marketing directed at children would figure so prominently in a book about financial planning. Chapter Three, "Groomed to Consume," speaks to the important role that child marketing plays on our personal finances. If you were born after 1970 or have children who were born after 1970, you will want to pay special attention to this chapter. This chapter will examine the marketing assault that has been directed at children and the financial consequences that have, for the first time in history, recently come to light. According to marketing professor James McNeal, a leading expert and author on marketing to children, children only started to be considered consumers in the 1980s. It was at this time that companies began realizing that children had not yet been exploited and that children could be spoken to rather than marketing just to Mom. The marketing industry shifted and decided to target them directly. According to a former employee of a major marketing firm, it "was a conscious effort to move to direct kid marketing and not even worry about Mom. Just take her out of the equation." (4) The financial consequences of a generation of children who have been "groomed to consume" are many. There is an increasing amount of pressure on family spending, and many children grow up with little to no financial education. The frightening part of this story is that many of us do not even know how and by whom our financial beliefs and values have been shaped. As psychologist and author Robert Cialdini points out, "Once we have made up our minds about an issue, stubborn consistency allows us a very appealing luxury: We really don't have to think hard about the issue anymore. We don't have to sift through the blizzard of information we encounter every day to identify relevant facts." (5) This chapter will assist you in identifying which factors have shaped and are shaping your financial belief structures so that you might attempt to counter their influence in your life.

The fourth chapter, "Spending to Belong and the New Necessities: The Second Assassin," speaks to a Swedish proverb that states that "If you buy what you don't need, you steal from yourself." This chapter is therefore designed to help you stop stealing from yourself. It will expose the second Money Assassin: marketing and advertising. Since the 1970s, the marketing and advertising industries have undergone a significant transformation and now play a major role in both our personal and financial lives. Through intense consumer research, marketers have gained valuable insights into all aspects of our spending, including information on where, what, when, how, and why we buy. In short, marketers understand aspects of our financial psyche better than we do—we cannot escape their agenda and this has not fared well for our bank accounts. In examining the role of marketers and advertisers in our lives, this chapter will also explore their intense branding campaigns, product placements, and secret undercover marketing strategies that make it extremely difficult for us to break free of the social pressures and expectations to consume. After reading this chapter, it will become clear how this social pressure has created the risk and fear of social exclusion. Understanding our consumer society and the new role marketing and advertising play in our lives is a fundamentally important step in breaking free of debt and critical to the achievement of financial well-being.

The central message throughout this book is that many of the financial struggles we face in our lives are the result of our lifestyles and the economic environments in which we live, and not due to our lack of understanding of how compound interest works or some other financial theory or strategy. Don't get me wrong, it is important to understand the basics of personal financial theory and planning;

however, a prerequisite to a life of financial well-being is a solid and healthy financial belief structure. I have therefore invested a great deal of time and energy in trying to understand and present you with the complex factors that drive our financial behaviour. With this knowledge, awareness, and clarity under your belt, you will be ready to explore the more specific "financial" rules and guidelines, as I have outlined and explained in the second part of this book.

The second part of the book focuses on three specific aspects of your personal finances: your vehicle, home, and personal debt. Part two concludes with a chapter that focuses on pearls of financial wisdom including how much one should be committing to their financial plan and how it should be designed. I have chosen to focus on the vehicle, home, and personal debt in particular because many of us tend to overextend ourselves in one of these areas, making it extremely difficult to find additional money from other areas to help our cash flow. The graph below represents the expenses incurred for a typical family:

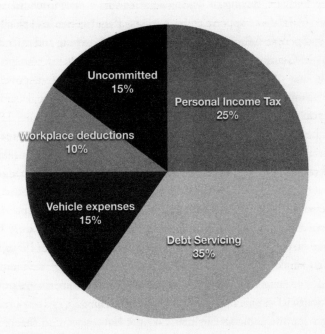

In looking at the typical expenses incurred as revealed by the graph, it is easy to understand why many of us, with only 15 percent of our budget left to spend on children, vacations, hobbies, entertainment, food, and our financial plan, are spending more than we make. The result is increased levels of debt and no savings. Throughout the book, you will be asked to calculate your own personal numbers, using the *Money Assassins* website *www.moneyassassins.com*. This is an important exercise, as it enables you to determine your personal figures and ratios and will help you make improvements where they are needed. As you will note in reading the chapters in the second part of the book, I have outlined specific and practical ways to free up money so that more can be allocated and committed to eliminating debt and creating wealth.

In Chapter Five, "Living Car-Lite: The Discovery of Free Money," we will examine the costs of vehicle ownership as well as the financial benefits of making the transition to adopting a "car-lite" lifestyle. Contrary to the multi-billion-dollar-a-year automobile advertising campaigns that tell us that a vehicle can deliver prestige, power, and sex, buying or leasing a car can be a disastrous financial move. (6) It also happens to be a mistake that is made repeatedly, with few people fully aware of the true costs of owning and operating a vehicle. Gaining an understanding of the true costs of transportation is one of the easiest and most effective ways of discovering "free" money that will help you achieve your financial goals sooner than you thought possible.

Chapter Six, "Home Cent$," addresses perhaps the single greatest determinant of the long-term financial fate of an individual or family: the decision to buy a home. Although this decision has a tremendous impact on our financial well-being, 80 percent of first-time homebuyers never seek professional advice. It is important to note that previous generations were able to raise their families in homes that were half the size of today's, and at a fraction of the cost. During the 1950s, the "typical single-earner household allocated only 14% of its monthly income for an average middle-class home; starter homes were priced at about twice an average family's [annual] income." (7) Today, many garages are the same size as many of the homes were in the 1950s.

With housing expectations outstripping our income by three or four times, it is unrealistic to expect the average income earner to save any money. This chapter brings the financial reality of owning a home back to a responsible level. It provides guidelines on appropriate mortgage-to-income ratios, discusses the benefits of location efficiency, addresses how to manage the emotional buying process, and, for Canadian readers, brings to light the dangers of using the Home Buyers' Plan to fund a down payment. Ultimately, the goal of the chapter is to make the home buying process less overwhelming, less stressful, and more financially prudent.

Since the 1970s, debt has become an increasing burden on the vast majority of people's financial plans and an accepted, yet unnecessary, part of life. Debt is the third Money Assassin, as it kills most financial plans before they even leave the starting gates. The normalization of debt has resulted in financial hopelessness and dejection for many. Chapter Seven, "The Joy of Living Debt Free: Escaping the Third Assassin," explores ways to eliminate current debt and presents ways to avoid debt in the first place. It addresses the root cause of most debt—over-consumption—and guides you through the process of how to rebuild a debt-proof attitude toward your finances. You will be taken through an excellent exercise that will bring clarity to your core financial convictions and beliefs, which will result in a more debt-resistant outlook. We will calculate and have a detailed discussion about the importance of maintaining an appropriate total debt service ratio. I will also help dispel the "good debt" myth and tackle the common question of "Should I save or pay off debt?" Debt is a weight that hangs around the neck of many of us, draining valuable energy and wellness, ultimately preventing you from living the life you dream of creating. The goal of this chapter is to help relieve you of this weight so you can focus your valuable energy on those priorities and initiatives that bring you the most joy in life.

Chapter Eight, "Financial Wisdom," will outline some of the most critical components required to achieve financial success. This chapter will touch on the more traditional concepts of financial planning. It is at the end of this book because it is only of value if you have followed the advice outlined throughout the previous chapters and you are truly committed to saving the required amount for your financial future. This chapter will discuss the "Heart Attack Graph," a graph that will give you the most honest look of where you are and provide you with an excellent prediction of your likelihood of achieving financial success. I will also examine one of the most important concepts in the entire book, the investor-saver confusion, which helps us recognize if we have graduated from a saver to an investor. The world of personal insurance is one of the most neglected aspects of a financial plan yet can have severe and dire consequences if left unattended. This chapter will end by looking at why it is crucial that you protect your most priceless financial asset (yourself!) and how to go about doing so.

The book ends with a summary of the key ideas presented in *Money Assassins* and highlights the most important points to take away.

I wish you the courage and strength to defeat the Money Assassins, eliminate debt, and create the wealth and life you desire!

Best wishes,
Chad Viminitz

Chapter 1

The Great Forgetting

Ours, one of the richest countries in the world, may be the poorest in terms of its collective financial memory. Perhaps the remembrances of survivors of a time past may serve as a reminder to others. Or to themselves.
— Stud Terkel, *Hard Times* (1)

He who does not know history is destined to remain a child.
—Cicero

Two of the most seminal events of the twentieth century were arguably the Great Depression and World War II. For most readers, these events bring up images of a Hollywood blockbuster film, or a few random names, dates, and places from a high-school history course taken way back when. While we might recognize the paramount role these events played in shaping the world in which we live today, for many readers it is our grandparents who experienced these hardships we must turn to in order to fully understand the implications of these events. Although much change occurred during our parents' time, it is in revisiting the wisdom and ways of those who suffered through the Depression and the Second World War that we might relearn and truly comprehend the financial lessons that past generations learned from these shocks. As the ancient Roman philosopher Cicero reminds us, in understanding our history, we may move forward.

Daniel Quinn, author of the critically acclaimed and award-winning bestselling novel *Ishmael,* writes that "the cultural self-awareness we inherit from our parents and pass on to our children is squarely and solidly built on a Great Forgetting." (2) In his book, *The Story of*

B, Quinn refers to society's forgotten transformation from a hunter-gatherer society to Neolithic farming communes, villages, towns, and, ultimately, kingdoms. "What was forgotten in the Great Forgetting was the fact that, before the advent of agriculture and village life, humans had lived in a profoundly different way."

It is my belief that a similar, though admittedly less profound, forgetting has occurred today with respect to our attitudes, perspectives, and behaviours towards personal finance. In understanding our financial history, lessons can be learned about the power of a society with a shared mission as well as the positive role that our governments can play in our struggle and quest for financial well-being.

Those who grew up during and lived through the 1930s and '40s became the greatest savers in modern financial history. World War II and the Great Depression helped shape a generation to view and perceive money in a fundamentally different way than previous generations, altering their financial psyche and generating in them a deepened appreciation for thriftiness, frugality, and the need to avoid debt. The end outcome was a new generation of savers with a thirst for financial prudence and an unprecedented accumulation of wealth.

If building a solid financial foundation is your goal, it is essential that you fully realize and appreciate that there are many different ways of living your financial life that differ from today's financial status quo. Our society has forgotten that in days gone by, living without debt was expected. Back then a one vehicle family was the norm, a home was 1,000 square feet, thriftiness and frugality were praised attributes, marketers targeted adults not children, mortgages were a fraction of a person's salary, engagement rings were an expression of love not indebtedness, eating out was a special family event, rations were a part of life, and "waste not, want not" did not mean you were cheap.

Although it is to past generations that we must look in order to relearn financial lessons, I want to assure readers that I am not advocating a return to the lifestyles of the 1930s or '40s. The suggestions and strategies that I put forward in this book do not call for a return to the devastating living conditions that existed for some during the 1930s, but instead I hope to encourage readers to rediscover a financial mindset that was born out of the misery, struggles, and sacrifices of the time. What is often forgotten of this time is that another story emerges when we dig a little deeper. In many of the stories of the Depression, individuals describe the period as a time of freedom, liberation, sharing, excitement, cooperation, and creativity. One individual even recalled having "the best and healthiest summer" he could remember despite his financial hardships. (3) It is hard to imagine a period of such financial chaos as anything else but depressing, but it is necessary to realize that the picture that has been painted of this time is perhaps not entirely accurate.

A fundamental change occurred in the financial psyche of this generation. People emerging from that era realized that financial hardships could come about unexpectedly and that financial preparedness was therefore vital at the individual, family, and societal levels for the financial well-being of all. Today, we lack any degree of financial preparedness, and as a result we are vulnerable to factors outside of our control. We are left on our own to survive and figure out personal finances with little or no societal support.

No phrase better explains the outcome of the Great Depression than the oft-spoken adage "what doesn't kill us only makes us stronger." In the words of famous broadcast anchor Tom Brokaw, those who lived through the Depression and World War II are the "Greatest Generation." Can we replicate this greatness that is being lost with the passing of the survivors of the "hard times" of the Great Depression? I am confident that in studying our forgotten past, we may gain valuable insights into reducing debt and creating wealth, which may help get us back on the path to moving forward as a society.

"Hard Times"

The 1920s were a time of unstoppable wealth accumulation with everyone from all walks of life participating. The 1920s' stock market rise not only made headline news, it penetrated and helped shape the 1920s culture. Fortunes were being made by the masses and the widespread belief was that the "Roaring '20s" would never end. The following quotation highlights the atmosphere of the day: "The idea of the stock market quittin' was unbelievable. Only naïveté permitted us to believe this could go on forever...." (1) As with any financial boom, no individual wanted their family to be left behind. The temptation to get rich quickly was difficult to resist in the gold rush–like climate of the day. Farmers, janitors, construction workers, doctors, and lawyers jumped on the stock market bandwagon with hopes of getting rich, fuelled by "experts" who promised and falsely predicted that the stock market was a safe and secure place to make money.

In the late 1920s, prominent politicians, businessmen, and academics proclaimed: "There is no cause for worry. The high tide of prosperity will continue."(4) Even a cheerful President Herbert Hoover proclaimed: "We shall soon with the help of God be within sight of the day when poverty will be banished from the nation." (5) But it was in the autumn of 1929 that Yale economist Irving Fisher made his immortal estimate that stock prices had reached a permanently high plateau. Universal shock was felt by the public in the fall of 1929 when the most intelligent, "in the know," and well-intended individuals were proven dreadfully wrong. The market crashed beyond belief. October 24th, 1929 would go down as the day that sent the economy and stock market into a downward spiral, thus triggering the beginning of the Great Depression. Millions of financial lives, perceptions, and behaviours would be challenged and changed forever.

The long-lasting effect of the crash of 1929 lingered in the memory of those who experienced the hardships of the time. Many who endured the Depression use descriptors such as *debilitating, intense, traumatic, vivid, horrendous,* and *devastating* to describe their experiences. One survivor said, "My habit of life has been changed by the Depression...these wounds are permanent." (1) Others referred to these memories as "invisible scars," scars that left their marks in their minds and, more specifically, on their financial belief systems. They were forced to internalize and re-examine the fundamental purpose of personal finance. This re-examination led to a financial mindset or psyche rooted in saving, thrift, and frugality that stayed with them forever. Till this day, many of those who lived through this time strictly respect their budgets and practice great financial restraint.

The tone of the Great Depression can be summed up in one word: FEAR—Fear of money, business, people, and possessions reigned during this time. (1) Fear also transformed financial behaviours and values, with fear of another depression ultimately driving many to view debt as evil. They ferociously saved for self-protection, resulting in a national savings rate of 10 percent, a rate that has never been equalled. In comparison, the national savings rate in Canada and the United States has been in a tailspin over the past two decades and currently hovers around 0 percent, with occasional rates dipping below 0.

A clear distinction that must be made at this point is the difference between saving and investing. I hope you noticed that I have been using the word *save* rather than *invest*. I believe there is a critical distinction between these two terms and will explore the important difference in another chapter in the section entitled "The Investor-Saver Confusion." However, in the context of our discussion about financial lessons to be learned, what ultimately must be retained from the post–Great Depression years is that "wealth accumulation or getting rich" took a back seat to saving out of fear of another economic collapse.

A cause for serious concern is a return to the blind illusions of "experts" that good times are here to stay. We mistakenly believe that we are smarter than previous generations and that we can foresee any economic trouble ahead and make the adjustments in time—a perfect example is the recent credit crisis. Just like the 1920s and '30s, our experts, predominantly led by an army of economists, tell us not to worry about our record levels of debt and reassure us that a low savings rate is of little concern. While economists look at the economy for a measure of success, individuals look at their quality of life, which are two fundamentally different ways of viewing financial well-being. Ours is a society that believes that science, technology, or economic savvy is one step ahead of menacing disaster. The famous Harvard economist John Kenneth Galbraith once wrote that during economic prosperity we are all financial geniuses. It is only after the fall, in hindsight, that we realize our obvious errors in judgment.

To suggest that our experts and leaders never get it right is, of course, a gross exaggeration. To believe that human ingenuity provides a force field from any large-scale potential future problems is simple ignorance. The variables and global factors at hand suggest that addressing any potential problems will be a daunting task. Though I do not pretend to be able to foresee or predict when or if another financial disaster may be on the horizon, many leading voices have sounded the alarm. Former Senior Vice-President and Chief Economist at the World Bank Nicholas Stern warns in the Stern Review that if the economics of climate change are not addressed, an economic crisis on the scale of the Great Depression is possible. Others warn of the end of cheap energy, including oil, as a catalyst or tipping point to severe economic hardship or the potential financial impact that could result from terrorist attacks.

While economic challenges may not be new to us, the way in which we handle them is. During the past few decades, we have survived economic turbulence by incurring personal debt. The availability of credit cards, lines of credit, and home lines of credit have allowed individuals to maintain the perception of "doing alright." Meanwhile, as a collective, we have reached record levels of debt, levels that we may soon realize have maxed out. Our short financial memory and blindness to economic fear make us vulnerable. This inability to understand the seriousness of the situation is further damaged by a frenzied marketing industry that is fuelling excessive consumption, thus resulting in the prioritization of consumption over savings. In another chapter, I will describe how consumption, which is mainly funded by debt, has been mistakenly confused with savings as a means to obtaining economic security.

Today's financial mindset is significantly different from that of the pre-1970s, when savings trumped consumption. The explosion of easy access to debt since the 1970s has been the main instigator in creating an environment that quickly and easily erases our financial memory. In a temporary and selective role, debt can assist in avoiding another Depression and help protect the family lifestyle during difficult times, yet it is our recent chronic dependency on it that has severe consequences for both our societal and individual well-being.

Readers might be asking, won't the current credit and economic crisis force or change our behaviour? Sadly I say no, because these recent events have not shaken individuals to their philosophical or psychological core, and without introspection, no meaningful change will occur. Another reason is that for society to have this type of transformation, all classes must be severely affected economically.

Survivors of the Depression have never forgotten those defining years and the impact they had on their lives. Yet with the passing of this generation, we are in jeopardy of losing a piece of our history and the accompanying financial value system. Most financial advisors are not aware of the critical role of the Depression in the development of the financial planning industry, nor are they aware of the profound transformations that occurred in the financial minds and behaviours of a generation. As I hope you will see by the end of this book, people's financial lives have been shaped in a profoundly different way since the 1970s. Today, the "lingering effect" of economic hardship has been forgotten and with it the lessons learned and the realization that "hard times" can be just around the corner. If the Great Depression is to teach us anything, it must be to acknowledge our vulnerability in a complex and ever-changing financial system. Ultimately, we must remember the need to protect ourselves financially, but that in large part is a matter of choice.

A Shared Mission

The depth of the economic impact of the Great Depression was far-reaching, as nearly everyone from all walks of life scraped by to provide food and shelter for their families. Financial hardship was on display for everyone to see. A financial levelling of sorts occurred, since no social class or occupation was exempt from financial devastation. Stories of lawyers starving, university professors unable to afford eggs, accountants digging ditches, and young boys' paper routes being the most important job in the family were not unusual. Even one doctor, who could not get a job after his internship, was turned away from a small town because the townspeople did not believe that a doctor was unable to get a good job in a larger centre. (3)

As the Depression penetrated all corners of society, a sense of empathy for one another was generated, particularly in terms of one's financial situation. Responsibility for an individual's financial hardship was no longer simply the fault of the individual, as the downtrodden came to be seen to some extent as victims of an uncontrollable and complex economic system. This shared empathy and commitment to help one another also translated into helping rebuild each other's financial foundations.

An excellent example of how society was able to financially rebuild itself was demonstrated in the practice of rationing. Rationing was an accepted part of life and "waste not, want not" became a national slogan that captured the attitude toward consumption. It is interesting to note the changing definition of the word *consume* over time, as it once referred to exhausting, pillaging, laying waste, and destroying. In fact, the word also had a medical connation as the term *consumption* was previously used synonymously with the infectious disease tuberculosis. (6) Tragically, rationing, a practice that was once heralded as nation-building and an effective means to achieve financial well-being, is now regarded as a practice of the plight of the poor.

Although financial struggles may affect many different social classes today, what has been lost is our sense of empathy toward each other, as we no longer feel any camaraderie with others in society. Our networks of support have disappeared and we must now go it alone in times of financial turbulence. Furthermore, our hardships are masked with debt loads that are invisible to our friends and colleagues, restricting others' ability to show concern or empathy. We now feel a sense of isolation and failure, and have returned to the belief that personal hardships are an indication of an individual's lack of motivation, discipline, or some other shortcoming.

During the Depression, hundreds of thousands of people felt the burden of hard times, though there were others who internalized feelings of economic failure and blamed themselves. The majority did not share this feeling of shame, as they recognized the complexity of the situation. What changed during the Depression was the belief that hard work and self-discipline alone did not guarantee success; individuals learned that they were vulnerable to outside forces that were beyond their control. This sense of responsibility for financial failure has evolved over time, as revealed in the following quotation from a survivor of the Depression: "There just wasn't any of that...Today you're made to feel it's your fault. If you're poor, it's only because you're lazy and you're ignorant, and you don't try to help yourself." (1)

As we will explore in the next chapter, social forces and the financial environment in which we live play a significant role in our consumption choices. Although, I firmly believe that personal choice plays a vital role in determining the financial success of an individual, to completely disregard the environmental factors at hand and the influence they exert on our thoughts and behaviours is simply unrealistic. To use an analogy, I find it extremely hard to believe that over 50 percent of the general population has consciously chosen to be overweight and out of shape, leading to some of the highest levels of diabetes in history and what could be considered an epidemic. Surely parents want the best for their children and would not willfully choose dangerously high levels of childhood obesity and the associated health ramifications for them. Personal choice plays a role in our health, but more and more research shows that the complex interplay of economic, social, and environmental factors are increasingly influencing our choices in determining our overall well-being. Clearly our perspectives on health have been drastically altered by the way we eat, the size of our portions, our levels of exercise, and the quality of air we breathe. These changes have gradually evolved, often without our full knowledge or consent. Our financial well-being has also been shaped by factors that we may not be aware of nor have consented to.

It is no coincidence that the generation that lived through the Depression developed many of today's social safety nets. In Canada, for example, Old Age Security (1952) and the Canada Pension Plan (1965), as well as a publicly funded health care system were products of this generation. These and other programs enjoyed today are direct outcomes of a generation with a deepened sense of empathy, a real understanding that "hard times" can hit us all, and a shared mission to develop effective measures to provide support across class divisions. It is also interesting to note that increased savings by the middle class resulted in their increased share of the nation's wealth. As the wealth of the top 0.5 percent of U.S. households shrank, the growing middle class witnessed an increase in wealth. We must keep in mind that during the 1940s, '50s, and '60s, redistribution of wealth was seen as a sign of progress and "economic strength and prosperity." Today, wealth distribution and disparity have returned to 1929 levels. (8)

Getting back to the idea of a shared mission, what is important to note is the absence of a common struggle. While the survivors of the Great Depression and WWII rallied around a concrete and clear challenge, there is no consensus today of what might constitute a shared financial mission. In striving for personal financial independence, we have been blinded to the trade-off between personal freedom and community. Once again, we must remember that an important part of the success of the greatest generation of savers can be found in the support from their peers and communities. Ties to families, neighbourhoods, and workplaces provided social approval and encouragement to live in keeping with their values. Living a life of thrift and frugality was viewed as an act of patriotism and did not suggest at all that the individual was cheap. This is just another reason why today's economic challenges are very different. Patriotism of the past encouraged saving, thrift, and frugality. These principles have been replaced with spend, consume, and spend and consume more!

While some may view the "War on Terrorism" or the fight against global warming as our new shared missions, few individuals have committed themselves to saving hundreds of dollars of their own money to add to these efforts. In fact, governments have asked their citizens to do just the opposite—to show our support, we should spend and consume. As for global warming, there is little evidence to suggest that we are truly committed to change our current collective lifestyle to curb climate change, though I hope to be proven wrong. I do, however, strongly believe that humans are innately compassionate and giving and that we will often move mountains for our family, friends, and even acquaintances before pursuing our own selfish motives. It is this feeling that guides my belief in the need to develop a new shared mission that enables us to step back from the consumer culture that is toxic to our society and instead re-evaluate our financial behaviour.

The developing of sound habits of saving by those who experienced the Depression, and even more so, those who experienced World War II, can largely be explained by the active encouragement and marketing by the government to promote saving. The government during the war needed money to fund the war effort, and to secure this money, the Victory Bonds marketing campaign was used. This campaign came at a time when politicians were in the process of reviewing the legitimacy of companies writing off their advertising expenses. This potential blow to the advertising industry necessitated a coming together of the industry to demonstrate their worthiness and ensure that their tax status was maintained. Designing government war propaganda to contribute to the war effort was seen as the solution. (9) In this case, advertising played a positive role in securing financial well-being. Victory Bond posters used such slogans as: "The least I can do! – Is to buy Victory Bonds," in which we see a picture of a man working in a factory who is trying to appeal to the men who did not go off to war. Other posters portray men fighting abroad using slogans such as: "Back Him Up! – Buy Victory Bonds." The poster that I find most fascinating shows Adolf Hitler whispering into a woman's ear as she pulls some money out of her purse. The caption reads: "Go on, spend it...what's the difference?" The caption on the bottom reads: "National Thrift is essential....And Thrift begins with those little things you needlessly buy from day to day....saving to buy War Savings Stamps is a vital war job for every woman, man and child...let THRIFT be your watchword!" When can you recall your government telling you that thrift and rations were your civic duty?

Our governments subscribe to a system that encourages us to consume as the stakes are high to do so. In 2007, Statistics Canada stated, "Consumer spending is a key contributor to a country's economic health." In fact, consumer spending represents between 60 percent of Canada's Gross Domestic Product (GDP) and represents upwards of 70 percent in the United States. As individual consumption habits play such a central role in a country's economic growth, any increase in the personal savings rate reduces the total amount that could otherwise be used for consumption. The end result is an economic growth level in jeopardy of decline. At the heart of re-election is the need for a proven track record in creating a strong economy. As our economic system is designed today, a "healthy" economy requires consumer confidence, consumer spending, and new housing starts. That both our government and business community thrive on high levels of consumerism shows the unlikelihood of serious opposition emerging about high levels of consumption. Although lip service is often paid, there is too much at stake for those parties involved to take any real measures to address the financial situation in which our society finds itself. The hit political drama *The West Wing* captured this reality perfectly. When asked: "We don't want people to save or reduce their personal debt?" President Bartlet replied: "We do, but when the next guy is president."

The greatest generation of savers passed along simple and effective, tried and true "Golden Rules" for financial success: spend less than you make, save for a rainy day, avoid debt, help your neighbour, and do not desire more than you can use. Ironically, in the information age, where society has more access to financial education and advice than ever, we have largely ignored the proven methods and broken the most basic financial rules established by the generation that survived the Depression. As I noted earlier, it was the breaking of these most simple rules that started my quest for answers and led me to the Money Assassins. Our perspectives on wealth and financial well-being have been the first areas hijacked by the Money Assassins and it is to this transformation that we will now turn our attention.

Chapter 2

Wealth, Happiness, and the First Assassin

Beware an act of avarice; it is a bad and incurable disease.
—Ancient Egyptian Proverb

A man was fishing off the end of a pier when a stranger approached him. The stranger, struck by the fact that the fisherman was fishing from the pier, suggested that the fisherman buy himself a boat. The fisherman, surprised by such a comment, replied, "To what purpose?"

"Well, with a boat you could go where there were more plentiful and larger fish to catch," replied the stranger. Perplexed, the fisherman asked why he would want to do that. The stranger, surprised by the fisherman's response, replied, "With more and larger fish than you need, you could sell the excess and use the money to further increase the size of your boat. And in doing so, could not only increase your harvest but could increase your financial returns even further by processing your catch and then marketing directly to consumers."

The fisherman, confused by such a proposal, looked up at the stranger, and again replied: "Why would I do all that you say?"

The stranger, dumbfounded by the fisherman's simple-mindedness, replied, "In doing so, you would become a wealthy man who could afford to go fishing any time you wanted."

And to this, the fisherman replied, "I already can."

The key to financial success and finding happiness lies in first understanding what it is we are seeking. Humankind's pursuit of both wealth and happiness has been shrouded in mystery, confusion, and irony. While the secret to finding happiness may be rather complex and uncertain, the same cannot be said for accumulating wealth. Although the term *wealth* is itself rather arbitrary, the formula to create it is surprisingly simple. While the path to financial success may come as a disappointment to some, since it is not as easy to find as we may have hoped for, the math is as basic as can be: spend less than you make! But for all its simplicity, this most basic of rules is under attack as our perceptions of wealth, the pursuit of money to buy happiness, and the Money Assassins are undermining our ability to live by this rule.

Canadians currently spend more than they make, clearly violating the most basic financial rule. Spending less than you make is a proven and logical method for financial success, but it is proving to be extremely difficult for many to achieve. The reason why we are struggling to live by this rule is that to do so we must live within constraints, make difficult choices, and prepare and plan for the future. We have instead turned to a new alternative way that promises freedom, security, and happiness, under the illusion that wealth and happiness can be achieved with little to no work or sacrifice. Unfortunately, as a result of our consumerism and materialism, chronic financial anxiety, fear of social alienation, and a life of financial indebtedness are wreaking havoc on our lives.

In this chapter, we will explore the constantly changing definition of wealth, focusing on our own perceptions while revealing how these perceptions act as a driving force for our consumptive behaviour. We will also examine one of the most misleading myths that is being propagated today: that famous equation that money equals happiness. In the last part, you will meet the first assassin, technology, and come to realize how technological advances serve to further enslave us financially. Hold on, we're going for a ride!

The Perception of Wealth

> *The utility of consumption as an evidence of wealth...is well established in men's habits of thought.*
> —Thorstein Veblen, *Theory of the Leisure Class* (2)

When people say they want to be rich or wealthy, what do they really mean? Do they aspire to have a million dollars, three homes, or do they just want a life of leisure? The Great Depression and the two World Wars forced past generations to take a hard look at what they truly wanted in life, instilling in them a clear sense of their motives, goals, and values. In conversations today, there is an overall lack of discussion about the role that money plays in our lives. Instead, our financial discussions centre on investment strategies, rate of return, and early retirement.

In his book *The Economics of Happiness* ecological economist Mark Anielski examines the history and meaning of the word *wealth*. Although most dictionaries currently define wealth using monetary terms such as *money* and *property*, this has not always been the case. Anielski reveals that *wealth* literally means "the conditions of well-being" and that according to the Greek language "wealth is a means to or way of being well." (3) These former definitions of wealth have failed to survive the test of time largely as a result of the way in which economic well-being and growth are measured today. It is my opinion that we ought to return to Anielski's description of wealth, as it recognizes values outside of work and consumption. Aristotle regarded the pursuit of wealth, property, power, reputation and status, as "external goods" and markers of success. (16)However, Aristotle also considered fortitude, temperance, justice, and wisdom to be "goods for the soul." In his view, happiness belonged to those who could cultivate "their character and mind to the uttermost, and…" who could keep their "acquisition of external goods within moderate limits." (16) An imbalanced pursuit of both "external goods" and "goods for the soul" prevents us from fully reflecting on our lives and the choices that we make. This state of imbalance is precisely the situation in which today's consumer society finds itself.

Most of today's economists measure wealth and progress through narrowly defined measures such as gross domestic product (GDP). Although GDP remains the most dominant measure in use, it fails to factor in costs such as health (physical or mental), debt, quality of life, or environment. To illustrate this shortcoming, one of the most devastating environmental disasters, the 1989 Exxon Valdez oil spill, increased GDP. Labour, travel, lawyer fees, studies, media coverage, and other clean up efforts led to increased spending, which is great for fuelling GDP growth. This is a shocking example of the ridiculousness of this measure. Another example that highlights the skewed reality in using the GDP as a measure of "progress" is the fact that the current obesity epidemic is regarded as a significant contributor to growth in GDP. Paradoxically then, devastating damage to both the health of our environment and our bodies are some of the driving forces in a stronger and healthier economy.

Alternative measures that take into account growth, wealth, and cost also exist, such as the genuine progress indicator (GPI). While undertaking research for this book, I came upon a startling figure. Both GDP (the traditional economic index) and GPI (an alternative index) followed side by side during the 1950s and '60s, which suggests that economic growth resulted in an overall higher standard of living. However, a divergence occurred in the early 1970s: GDP continued to climb while GPI began to fall. This divergence suggests that traditionally measured economic growth in the form of increased consumption does not result in a higher standard of living. Rather, this divergence may indicate that our society is on the alarming path of achieving a lower overall standard of living.

Changing habits within our consumer society have quietly reshaped our road to wealth. Whereas accumulation of wealth was once a benchmark for financial success, we now settle for the quick fix of achieving the perception of having wealth. This perception of wealth is much more attainable and exciting than real accumulation, as it is rooted in the self-gratifying world of consumption and immediate gratification. The desire to achieve the perception of wealth was first revealed in surveys undertaken by the University of Michigan in the 1980s. (12) These surveys revealed that for many individuals, the perception of wealth mattered more than real monetary wealth. As we will see throughout the course of this chapter, the need to be perceived as having wealth has overtaken our ability to recognize the importance of achieving real financial stability and security.

Subscribing to a value set that necessitates constraint, discipline, and planning now seems old-fashioned, dated, and feels like a return to hard times. At first glance, new alternatives to wealth, such as consumption and riskier investments, come across as very attractive—

until you read the fine print—for in choosing this path, we soon come to realize that this road leads over a financial cliff. We are shocked to discover the illusiveness of the end of the road, as there is no end in sight but rather a constantly changing mirage. The pursuit of the perception of wealth misleadingly directs us down dead-end roads such as spending to belong, consumptive communities, and relative consumption, otherwise known as "Keeping up with the Joneses." No warning bells are triggered when we start to tread along this path of consumption, and there is no mention of the sacrifices that will be made to our leisure time, personal health, family relationships, and natural environment. In essence, this notion of wealth requires us to neglect the real wealth that in many ways we already have, such as time, health, and family and friends. Who among us is like the fisherman in the fable, able to recognize the wealth we already have?

If many of us are seeking the perception of having wealth and are not pursuing actual wealth, what does this really mean? Simply put, the primary objective of the perception of wealth is to either have more than we had in the past or have more than others have now. When incomes are stagnant, which has been the case for the majority of North Americans for the past few decades, this first option is not available. Whereas our occupation and income historically served as markers of wealth and social standing, the same cannot be said today. According to John Kenneth Galbraith, author of *The Affluent Society,* wealth and income alone no longer carry the same prestige as they once did. Maintaining and increasing our social position or status now requires *evidence* of property and money. Evidence of actual wealth is now a perception, demonstrated by the quantity and quality of our consumption, our abstention from labour, and, more recently, by the establishment of high-profile private foundations and charities. (2) It is now this *evidence* of wealth, as perceived by others through our consumption, that serves as a financial yardstick of success. Although we may not fully realize that our consumption and overt spending are used as measurements of our financial well-being, the new reality is that to be perceived as having wealth, we must spend, often beyond our means.

Our increased access to higher levels of credit has fuelled much of our "evidence" or social status spending. Before the 1970s, when credit was limited, we had more constraints and thus rarely were we able to spend more than we made. Given the invisible nature of financial well-being, many have taken to displaying their goods in order to portray themselves as financially successful. The triad of goods that are most often used to demonstrate our wealth are our homes, vehicles, and wardrobes. Research backs this claim by revealing that Canadians spend more money on clothing "than they do on any other non-food item." (1) This is a rather logical way of effectively presenting ourselves in a desired financial light, as our clothing provides an immediate idea about our economic standing. We are all aware of the fact that we only get to make a first impression once, and so we make it count the first time around. To present ourselves in a certain financial light, we often resort to borrowing money to "purchase" our social standing and status. Meanwhile, we neglect to consider the impact that our behaviour is having on our financial security.

The historical markers of social status were traditionally occupation and income; however, these markers no longer carry the same level of prestige they once did. These historical markers served as yardsticks, since, until recently, limited access to credit required a well-paying job in order to adopt a certain lifestyle. These markers are clearly no longer measurements of our financial standing. I am often asked the following question: "I have friends who have expensive homes and cars, and travel more than I do...and they make less than I do. How can they afford it?" My answer to this question is always very simple: "Debt and no savings." Our access to credit enables people from a wide variety of social and economic backgrounds to attain levels of social mobility that were once not possible. The problem lies in the unsustainable nature of this social mobility. This drive for social mobility influences our levels of consumption, and ultimately debt, resulting in huge setbacks in our financial plans.

Wasteful Wealth

To be perceived as having wealth, our consumption must be "wasteful." In this context, "waste" is viewed as a way to communicate to those around us that we are in a financial position that allows us to be "wasteful" with our time, money, and lack of labour. In the early 1900s, Thorstein Veblen, economist and author of *The Theory of the Leisure Class*, recognized "waste" as a key factor in identifying wealth. According to Veblen, the "element of waste" must be common in both conspicuous leisure and consumption in order to demonstrate reputable wealth. In the first case, leisure "is a waste of time and effort" and in the second, consumption is a waste of resources. (2)

The way in which people spend both their time and money can reveal a great deal about their financial situation. The ability to be "wasteful" sends a clear message to others in society that their financial success allows them to adopt such financial behaviour. This may sound like a strange idea to many, but a closer look at the practice reveals its effectiveness. According to Veblen, this practice of "wasting" is only one way in which we are able to communicate our level of real or *perceived* wealth to others.

Let's look at a few examples to help us better understand this idea. Rising gas prices affect us all to some degree. However, while some buckle under the weight of increased oil and gas prices, others do not seem to take much notice. We are making a statement when we say, "I can still afford to travel by air or in a high-gas-consuming vehicle." Furthermore, that I can afford to spend money on frivolous benefits such as heated seats, a power sunroof, or a trim package says to the world that I have the resources to afford these high-priced luxuries. Our constantly growing use of both vehicles and airplanes means that we incur massive financial and environmental costs, even though a variety of more sustainable and cheaper alternatives exist. Interestingly, the use of high-heeled shoes by women was originally a statement of wealth, as it made even the most simple and basic manual or household chore extremely difficult. In wearing these shoes, these women were showing that they did not take part in household work, as they had the financial resources to pay others to do the work for them. (2) Another example is the process of turning gardens into lawns to send the message that "I don't have to grow my own food; I can afford to buy it and have someone else produce it." Without trying to pick on what is likely the favourite sport of some readers, golf is a case in point in communicating to others our financial well-being. There is a certain status associated with playing the sport, as it is often referred to as "a game for the rich." If an individual can afford to spend five or six hours away from work, it is fair to assume that a certain level of wealth enables this individual to indulge in what Velben would describe as "wasteful consumption." Although most of us are surely not motivated to play for appearance's sake, whether intended or not, those who play this game on a regular basis communicate to society that they are financially able to "waste" the required resources, time, and money to do so.

One of the most current and practical examples of Veblen's concept of waste is how today's children are learning about the three R's: reduce, reuse, and recycle. Yet for all of our wonderful attempts to help save the planet and practice the three R's, we neglect to abide by the rule: reduce, then reuse, and finally, if we cannot do the first two R's, recycle. Even though recycling is by far the least effective way and most resource intensive of the three, it gets all the attention. Recycling is really the perfect solution for most, as you get to keep consuming all that you want, without having to feel guilty about the true environmental consequences. The perception of wealth is kept intact by our ability to maintain high levels of consumption, while we live under the illusion that significant change is occurring through our advancements in recycling techniques. Speaking about the looming environmental problems, such as climate change, former Assistant Secretary General to the United Nations Robert Muller said, "The single most important contribution any of us can make to the planet is a return to frugality." (5) It is important to remember that many of today's riches are a result of the frugality of generations that came before us. If we are to pass on this wealth, we must learn to live more frugally. The challenge is to change a belief system that fails to recognize the virtues of frugality. As frugality is inherently non-wasteful, we are unable to communicate our wealth to others while living a life in line with the rules of being frugal. Until we can shed the belief that to be wealthy is to drive our vehicles and use excessive air travel, we will continue to live in a society that fails to see the real value in using a bike or public transportation.

For many of us today, to spend less than we make and to live a "rich life" requires us to live our lives in a fundamentally different way. In living this new life, we may also radically change our views about wealth and recognize that real wealth need not be wasteful. I think that I would go a step further and challenge ourselves to try and see beyond the traditional monetary and consumption parameters so often used to measure wealth. In coming together with our friends and families, and taking the time to examine what constitutes "conditions of well-being" and "goods for the soul," we may be able to develop a fuller and deeper meaning of wealth and get back onto the path to financial success.

Income and Happiness

Men do not desire to be rich, only to be richer than other men.
—John Stuart Mill

The gravest danger in the pursuit of the "perception of wealth" is the desire it creates in us to achieve increasing levels of income. The quest for greater income is rooted in the belief that with more income comes more opportunities to consume, resulting in increased levels of happiness and status. When and if we do come to realize the falsehood of this equation, we are often left frustrated, discouraged, and financially trapped.

One of the negative effects of our quest for perceived wealth is our need to spend more time at work to help pay for "Keeping up with the Joneses." Because we need to maintain an ever-increasing cash flow to keep pace with the new consumption standards, we look to loans, credit cards, and mortgages to fund the gap between stagnant incomes and rising consumption expectations. In our pursuit of greater cash flow, we tend to spend more time at work to help pay for this "desired lifestyle." Yet when surveyed, half of individuals are willing to trade a day's pay for a day off, 75 percent want to lead more simple lives and place less emphasis on material success, and two-thirds seek a greater balance between life and work. (5)(9)

Statistics Canada reported that one-third of 25- to 44-year-olds categorized themselves as workaholics, with many stating that they "felt trapped in a daily routine." (1) Michael Adams, social researcher and author of *Better Happy Than Rich?*, adds that the workplace has turned into a Darwinist jungle-like setting, resulting in diminishing job security and increased stress. Adams also describes the "frantic pursuit" of money as part of today's daily life, leaving "no time to stop and smell the roses." During the 1980s and '90s, the United Nations issued a report warning that workplace stress is "one of the most serious health issues of the 20th century."(7) Others have also warned of the dangers of being overly enthralled with the pursuit of money. In the words of John Wesley, spoken over three hundred years ago: "We should gain all we can but not at the expense of life nor at the expense of our health, nor without hurting our mind." (17)

I am perplexed by the contradictions I see around me. While we live in a society that highly regards our right to "freedom," many of us choose to imprison ourselves through our financial behaviour. On the one hand, we aspire to leading lives of wealth so that we may simplify our lives, spend more time with our families, take up hobbies, work less, and become more involved in our communities, while on the other hand, our actions lead us down a path that prevents us from doing any of the above. We are ultimately forced to increase our workloads and incur greater financial commitments.

Our ability to achieve financial well-being can only be realized once we recognize the true costs of pursuing the perception of wealth. We must also shatter the myth that increased levels of income will lead us to live happier lives. To do so, we must begin by re-evaluating the message that is being given to our youth. A study of children between the ages of 9 and 14 revealed that more than half of them agreed that "when you grow up, the more money you have, the happier you are." (14) Another study traced the changing perspectives regarding money over time amongst college students. In 1967, two-thirds of the students said that it was important to develop "a meaningful philosophy of life," while less than one-third said that "making a lot of money was important." Today, these figures have been reversed. (4)

While today's consumer culture and current economic system depend on a belief system that sees money as the key to happiness, the truth is that "much of human satisfaction takes place in the non-material domains, where objects are largely inconsequential." (10) Although we have all heard that "money does not buy happiness" and believe this on some gut level, many of us do not act or behave in a way that reflects this recognition. The academic community, notably in the social sciences, has undertaken research that confirms the notion that money does not buy happiness. Professor Robert Frank, author of *Luxury Fever*, found that "once a threshold level of affluence is achieved, the average life-satisfaction level...is essentially independent of its per-capita income," concluding that "no useful purpose is served by further accumulations of wealth." The "threshold level" of needed income has been debated, and ranges from $10,000 to $80,000, but is essentially reached once the basic needs of food, clothing, and shelter are met. (6)

Economists such as Noble Prize winner Daniel Kahneman and collaborator Alan Krueger have studied the question "whether more money or income buys more happiness?" They concluded that "the belief that high income is associated with a good mood (happiness) is greatly exaggerated and mostly an illusion." (3) One attitudinal study found that when respondents were asked to rate themselves as "very happy," "fairly happy," or "not very happy," the results changed very little between 1946 and 1970 despite an astounding 62 percent rise in real incomes during this period. (10) Other researchers explain that a rise in income fails to result in greater levels of happiness, as individuals are unable to foresee that an increase in income is accompanied by a desire for increased material goods. (3) Tim Kasser, psychologist and co-editor of *Psychology and Consumer Culture: The Struggle for a Good Life in a Materialist World*, even states that our desire alone to have more money can make us unhappy. It is hard to believe that even with all of this supporting evidence, our quest to achieve greater income with the goal of increasing our level of happiness continues, even after all of our basic needs have been met. The question needs to be asked, then, why do we insist and fervently believe that our pursuit of wealth will lead us to live fuller and happier lives?

As I mentioned in an earlier paragraph, we are taught at an early age to believe that money makes us happier. We are bombarded with sincere messages from our families, friends, and society at large to get good grades so that we can attend post-secondary education in order to get well-paying, secure jobs. We may have accepted this reasoning, but what if the basic assumptions are wrong? What we fail to understand is that income is no guarantee of financial success. This is a difficult statement to swallow, as this idea has been heavily promoted in society. Harvard University lecturer and best-selling author Juliet Schor discovered that the more income a person earns, the less they save. In one study, each increasing level of income corresponded with a reduction in annual savings. There is even some evidence to suggest that the more education a person has, the less they will save. This finding may come as a surprise to many, but can perhaps be explained by the fact that the more education a person has, the more likely they will be immersed or exposed to a "culture of upscale acquisition" or a more expensive consumptive peer group. I am not using this finding to suggest that the pursuit of higher education puts us at a financial disadvantage compared to those with less education, but rather to help demonstrate that greater income is no guarantee of financial success.

For years, the marketing industry and our consumer culture have been praising the virtues of materialism. While the above paragraphs clearly show that the secret to happiness cannot be uncovered in high rates of return, countless slogans tell us otherwise. Here are a couple of famous slogans to use as food for thought: "The one who dies with the most toys wins" and "Money isn't everything, but whatever comes second is a long way behind." These slogans clearly contradict the results from the genuine progress indicator that shows that happiness is not the by-product of the belief that more is always better. However, there is no doubt that having a higher income creates more opportunities to achieve financial success. Yet, as I described earlier, financial success can only be achieved when we spend less than we make. This is a phenomenon that current data and statistics reveal is clearly not occurring, even at higher income levels. Missing from the discussion on income is the reality that income satisfaction largely depends on how much others make, a concept known as relative income. Here is an example:

Ask yourself which annual salary would you prefer: $60,000 or $120,000. While I expect that everyone answered $120,000, you are surely waiting for the catch. Here it is. As research has shown, the preferred annual salary depends on the context. Let's look at two different hypothetical worlds with different income structures. Now choose which world you would prefer to live in. In the first world, World A, you will make $60,000 per year while others will make $30,000. In the second world, World B, you will make $120,000 per year while others make $200,000. If it is absolute income, which means that people desire more total income, we would expect most to choose to live in World B, where their annual income of $120,000 would be double that of World A. Interestingly though, when given the choice between these hypothetical worlds, the vast majority of people choose World A and its annual income of $60,000, a much lower level of absolute income compared to the $120,000 in World B. The key here, of course, is that the amount of money in World A represents a considerably higher level of income relative to their peers in World A. (6)

As the above exercise demonstrates, what matters most when it comes to income is how much we earn relative to others, not how much we earn in absolute terms. We therefore perceive our level of wealth and income through comparisons made with those around us. Joe Dominguez and Vicki Robin, authors of *Your Money or Your Life*, describe the race towards greater financial success, goods, or higher incomes as a mirage that can never be reached, as it is not real. We are unable to define what it is we are seeking, as our expectations about success constantly change as our relative social position and income change. This explains why the two-thirds of American households who make over $75,000 feel that they need an increase in income of 50 to 100 percent to be satisfied, while only "20% of those making $30,000 or less would need that much." (15)

As a collective, we are not experiencing greater happiness as a result of higher incomes. This occurs because although our expectations are being met from a consumption standpoint, overall well-being is not improving. Professor Barry Schwartz writes, "As long as expectations keep pace with realizations, people may live better but they won't feel better about how they live." (13) If we require a 2,200-square-foot home to feel financially successful, then any substantial raise in our income will likely be spent on upgrading our 900-square-foot condo to meet our "expectations" of ourselves and of society. However, although this catching up of sorts may give us an initial sense of satisfaction, this decision to upgrade will not translate into an increase of our financial well-being. In fact, according to Schwartz, as our consumption of goods transitions from pleasure to comfort, the result is often disappointment. For example, take the first time that you bought a car, a computer, or travelled abroad. Subsequent purchases or travels may not always provide the same degree of satisfaction as the first time, and may instead become commonplace. This disappointment is especially manifested in the consumption of "durable goods" such as vehicles, stereos, clothing, and computers. Simply put, as our incomes rise, our consumption of more expensive goods grows, and a sense of dissatisfaction and disappointment sets in. (13) Shifting our discussion away from income and happiness, we will now explore how one of the Money Assassins is making it easier and easier for us to consume, helping us try and "Keep up with the Joneses."

The First Assassin

> *Technological progress has merely provided us with more efficient means for going backwards.*
> —Aldous Huxley

> *We are becoming the servants in thought, as in action, of the machine we have created to serve us.*
> —John Kenneth Galbraith

During the 1960s and '70s, the future promised us great technological advancements that would provide us with the opportunity to work less and play more. U.S. President Richard Nixon, among others, proclaimed that a four-day work week would become the norm. The society of the twenty-first century would be changed by its abundance of personal leisure time. (8) I am sure many would agree that this envisioned society does not resemble the society that we live in today. As most people would recognize, we are instead working longer hours and have less and less time for ourselves.

In my research for this book, I was surprised to notice the role that technology played in many of the issues I was investigating. I quickly came to see how technology has influenced our ability to save money and spend within our means. In the coming chapters, we will come to see how technology has emerged as a Money Assassin, alongside today's consumer society and the world of debt. For now, though, we will briefly examine the direct impact technology has had on personal finance.

There is no doubt that technology has raised our standard of living through advancements in medicine, science, and innovation. However, greater choice, increased speed, and our new luxuries do not translate into raised levels of happiness or fulfillment nor do they result in financial well-being. Although technological advancements may be a progressive step forward in some areas of our lives, some advancements have also robbed us of the very benefits that they profess to provide to our financial well-being. It is therefore critical that we understand the role that technology plays in our financial lives in order to reclaim our financial independence.

Ultimately, technology has made it easier to spend beyond our means, as it has increased our desire to consume. Business has used technology to gain unprecedented access to data collection on consumer spending and preferences. Today's consumer tracking programs allow companies to identify and exploit emerging consumer trends and preferences, helping companies boost sales while pushing consumer spending to new levels. Technology has enabled products to move more quickly from the idea stage of development to the marketplace. Planned obsolescence of computers, cell phones, and other technologies force individuals to upgrade in order to keep up with the "Techno-Joneses." Although technology has played a large role in fuelling consumer spending, its largest impact has been in the transformation of our daily currency transactions and spending patterns.

Debit and credit cards have transformed our purchasing patterns by making impulsive and unconscious spending easier. This transformation has resulted in a general inability to save and an increased debt-load. Studies show that on average "people spend 23% more when they buy with credit cards than when they buy with cash." (5) It is mind-boggling to think of paying almost 25 percent more for every single purchase we make, not to mention the interest charges on top. Here is a very simple financial proposition: pay with cash and save 25 percent! Our hypnotic acceptance of the new techno-economy has left many of us unaware of the financial vulnerabilities we incur as a result of these new "conveniences."

Over a very short period, today's electronic monetary network has changed our payment or purchasing habits. Since the 1980s, cash's prominence as the preferred payment method has been in steep decline. Cash has been replaced by credit cards, debit cards, and now even cell phones. In 2000, Interac, a debit payment service in Canada, surpassed cash as Canadians' preferred method of payment after only ten years in the marketplace. It was only in 1993 that Sears began accepting major credit cards and was the last major retailer to do so. (11) It was also only in the 1980s that Visa and MasterCard began to have a reserved spot in our purses and wallets. Today's electronic financial network enables us to access monetary resources through a plethora of seemingly never-ending options. We are never prevented from spending and therefore do so with little consideration for our future financial well-being. I remember back in the late 1980s driving home with my parents and sister after racquetball practice when my dad suggested we stop and pick up Kentucky Fried Chicken (KFC) for dinner. My sister and I were excited, but neither my mom nor dad had cash with them. The ATM had just closed and KFC did not take Visa. As a result, we ended up driving home and having a much healthier and cheaper meal. This scenario would never happen today, as businesses, including fast food establishments, accept cash and virtually all types of plastic payment.

The benefits of plastic seem obvious: the convenience of payment, the need to no longer carry cash around, and the ability to circumvent any hassles with limited banking hours. What, then, is the problem? Isn't this just progress? *Webster's Dictionary* defines progress as "the advancement towards completion or maturity." However, since the introduction of these technologies in the 1980s and '90s, the financial behaviour of Canadians has been anything but mature, as we have deviated further away from our financial goals. Plastic has become today's currency and frivolous spending the new pastime. It has become commonplace to use debit cards for purchases under $10, a very costly additional expense, as this can increases the purchase price by 15 percent once the transaction fee is included. When you repeat this exercise a few hundred times a year, you can see why the banks are getting richer and your savings are going down! These changes in our financial behaviour have occurred so rapidly that we are only now beginning to realize their true costs.

The biggest danger that plastic poses to our financial well-being is its ability to bypass our financial conscience. Plastic enables us to buy into temptation, big or small, on an unlimited basis. Purchases go unchecked and the mystery of "where has my money gone?" goes unsolved. In a study of consumer use and attitudes towards credit cards, 75 percent of participants reported that cards tempt "one to buy more than is necessary" and that they make it too easy for them to purchase things they cannot afford. (11) Although we may be aware of the dangers at hand, many of us continue to dance with the "financial devil." We are persuaded by the actions of the crowd and participate without thinking twice about it. We are able to convince ourselves that our use of plastic is benign, as we proudly reason that "I don't pay any fees." But it is the real costs that are forgotten, or likely ignored, such as the impulsive, unnecessary, and frivolous purchases we make using our cards. *All* spending must be totalled, especially the spending that would not otherwise occur if plastic payment was unavailable. Remember that it is the $50 round of beers or the impulsive "just too good of a deal to pass up on" that are the real concerns in using today's financial technology and not the $1.50 transaction fee.

After the shopping euphoria subsides, buyer's remorse often sets in. We scold ourselves, saying, "I didn't really need that" or "if I was only more disciplined." This self-doubt and guilt serves to damage our self-confidence to manage our financial affairs. There is little to no financial education offered in our school system about the impact of technology on our financial well-being, with such education only becoming a requirement once we have hit or are close to hitting bankruptcy. When we become aware of the true costs of our methods of payment and level of consumption, we can overcome our often regrettable "in the heat of the moment" purchases. Practical solutions, such as using cash instead of plastic, might be challenging due to the pervasiveness and acceptance of debit and credit cards. Awakening and training our financial conscience to judge a purchase's validity will require some time and practice. However, when we use cash, we physically feel the money pass through our fingers. It awakens our conscience for a split second, creating a financial checkpoint at which we must either accept or reject the purchase. Cash also gives us an immediate and accurate up-to-date account of how much money we have left to spend, ensuring that we cannot spend more than we have! Plastic, on the other hand, fails to distinguish between our impulsive and necessary purchases, a distinction that can only be made by our financial conscience. As we are always looking for ways to find additional money, some simple rules will help us discover a way to get more. Never use debit cards for purchases under $20. Use cash for smaller purchases and cut out the hundreds of unnecessary purchases that are consuming your financial future. Using cash for larger purchases can also reduce spending by as much as 25 percent, a far greater rate of return than any investment. These simple rules clearly demonstrate that wealth accumulation is rooted in financial behaviour that is within your control.

Technological advances have helped enrich many aspects of our lives. Technology may serve to one day be a positive force in helping promote healthy financial behaviour. Until that day comes, we need to be aware of its potential to lead us down a financially dangerous road. As this chapter has shown, no demographic is immune to the mythology surrounding our perceptions of wealth, income, happiness, and the benevolence of technology. Studies have shown that many of our youth have already adopted these beliefs. In the next chapter, we will investigate in greater detail how a generation of children is being manipulated by a marketing industry that is specifically targeting them. In understanding how we are groomed to consume, we will be more equipped to challenge a system of myths about money that is damaging to both our personal and our families' financial well-being.

Chapter 3

Groomed to Consume

The kids we're reaching are consumers in training.... You want to reach consumers at their most formative point.
—Joseph Fenton, Educational Marketing Executive (1)

Kids are the most unsophisticated of all consumers; they have the least and therefore want the most. Consequently, they are in a perfect position to be taken.
—James McNeal, Retired Professor of Marketing at Texas A&M University (2)

In the first half of the twentieth century, the financial belief system of children that formed during their formative years was heavily influenced by frugal, debt-avoiding parents and a society that encouraged and praised financial constraint. David Korten writes, "They taught their children, use it up, wear it out, and make do or do without." (3) These financial virtues were passed along for generations. However, since the 1970s, these entrenched values and the financial golden rule of "spend less than you make" have been at best ignored and have at worst almost disappeared. One might think that finding the answer to why individuals are spending more than they are making should be simple, but nothing could be further from the truth. Few would suspect that the sum of the answers lie in the disturbing world of child marketing. Sending Money Assassins with their arsenal of weapons after an adult is one thing, but sending them after our children is an entirely different story. Understanding the impact of marketing toward children on our society is crucial to reclaiming the financial well-being of both parents and their children.

The concept and discussion of the involvement of children in consumer culture is neither new nor surprising. Many of us have fond memories of our childhood interactions at the neighbourhood grocery and candy stores. However, what is new is the shift in size and scope of children's influence on consumption. Today, 20 to 40 percent of purchases would not have occurred without the nagging of children. The role that children play in influencing their parents' consumption is significant. It is estimated today that the influence of children leads to an additional $600 billion in annual spending, as compared to only $5 billion in the 1960s. In light of these figures, it is obvious why children have been climbing to the top of the corporate agenda over the past 30 years. (2) Children's purchasing influence compels companies from a variety of grown-up industries to advertise on children's television networks. (5) For example, Nickelodeon, the television network giant, attempts to attract advertisers from the automotive industry, stating, "A nation of kids and they drive purchases; kids influence 62% of family SUV and minivan purchases." (5) The child marketing industry has clearly come a long way since the days of Cracker Jack!

The financial outcomes of child marketing are numerous. Children are raised in an environment where consumption overshadows savings. From an early age, children are groomed into accepting debt and spending beyond their means as ways of life. They are unconsciously manipulated to become brand loyal. The years of manipulation have far-reaching, long-term financial ramifications. Perhaps most alarming is that the damaging impact of child marketing is far from fully realized. According to child marketing expert James McNeal, selectively targeting children as consumers is a recent phenomenon, occurring only since the 1970s and '80s. (4) We are only now seeing the first generation of adults whose financial habits have been shaped by these practices.

With billions of dollars of profit at stake, marketers view children as company or product ambassadors who unknowingly deliver the corporate message to parents. Companies rely on these young ambassadors to influence parental spending and consumption. This undercover strategy has been highly successful though largely unrecognized within the public domain. It is very unsettling to believe that our children are being deliberately manipulated to steal from the family piggy bank in an effort to pad corporate bank accounts, increase stock prices, or gain market share. It is also difficult to reframe advertising as manipulative, given our fond memories of marketing campaigns such as Quaker's Life cereal's "Give it to Mikey, he'll eat anything" and "Mikey likes it!" or McDonald's catchy Big Mac jingles. However, as corporate profits expand, it is the family's financial future that incurs the adverse consequences.

In addition to the influence on family spending, children are unconsciously manipulated to become brand loyal, thus becoming lifelong customers. Companies believe that it is never too early to begin developing loyal customers, as branding influences purchasing right through adulthood. (6) A Nickelodeon study reported that over 90 percent of the purchase requests of children between the ages of 8 and 14 were brand specific, with almost all of the children stating that they tended to continue to use the same brand. Yet, the phenomenon of brand loyalty does not escape the adult demographic, especially in Canada, with over half of Canadians reporting that "the brand is very important to them" when making purchases. One executive refers to college students as future income streams. "If he [the student] turns out to be a big drinker, the beer company has bought itself an annuity," emphasizing the importance of the early development of brand loyalty. (7) However, it is clearly children who are most loyal, with research showing that children often recognize a brand logo before they can recognize their own name. (8) And if you are wondering if the advertisers' efforts are working, after the launch of the Budweiser Frog commercials in 1996, 73 percent of American children between the ages of 9 and 11 years identified that frogs say "Budweiser." (7) So let the race begin for companies to capture our children's loyalty, as no company can afford to let these potential future earnings slip through their fingers!

Branding is necessary, as it helps consumers distinguish between products. Although some consumers may be aware of this tactic, it is nevertheless easy for all of us to be manipulated. For example, at the request of my wife, I was recently sent off to buy some Tylenol. Although the pharmacist informed me of the availability of a significantly cheaper generic brand, I still bought the more expensive Tylenol. I was unable to shake off the brand loyalty I apparently have, despite the reassuring advice of a professional. Another example dates back to my preteen years, when at the age of twelve I was seeking my first Walkman. Sony had first entered the children's market in 1987 with their exciting "My First Sony" line. I purchased a Sony Walkman and, satisfied with my first Sony product, insisted upon purchasing a Sony stereo when the time came for an "electronic upgrade" a few years later. Naturally, when the time came to buy a receiver and a DVD player, I looked to the Sony family. It took a lot of my wife's convincing and some serious introspection before I was able to realize and accept that other brands also produce high quality and excellent value products. It was no easy battle to sever my preteen relationship with Sony and an experience that revealed a lot about the power and grip of brand loyalty.

Successful marketing occurs when marketers are able to communicate to their targeted audiences without individuals becoming aware that they are being marketed to. (7) While many parents might question the extent to which this targeting affects their families, a stark reality is revealed through the comments of marketing executives. In the eyes of the elite in the world of advertising, children are perceived in a much different light, and are viewed as "evolving consumers." Such executives highlight the financial need to "capture" them. (1) When Lucy Hughes, former Vice President, Director of Strategic Research for Initiative Media, one of the world's largest communications management companies, was asked if marketing to children was ethical, she bypassed the question, stating "I don't know." According to Ms. Hughes, her job was simply to move products, and if this was accomplished then she had done her job. (1)

In Juliet Schor's book, *Born to Buy*, Nancy Shalek, president of a leading marketing agency, is quoted as saying, "Advertising at its best is making people feel that without their product, you're a loser. Kids are very sensitive to that. If you tell them to buy something, they are resistant. But if you tell them that they'll be a dork if they don't, you've got their attention. You open up emotional vulnerabilities and it's very easy to do with kids because they're the most emotionally vulnerable." (5) Schor was shocked by Shalek's frankness when describing the exploitation of kids' vulnerabilities. It is clear that such executives and their firms seek to "own," "brand," and "capture" children, using strategies such as viral marketing and covert messaging. The combative and predator-like tones in which marketing executives describe strategies for child marketing is very troubling—no parent wants to hear these chilling terms being used in the context of their children.

Direct marketing to children is not the only tactic used by advertisers to increase family consumption. Parental authority has also been under attack in order to undermine the authority of parents over their children. The keynote address at "Kid Power," a marketing conference held in Disney World in 1996, was entitled "Softening the Parent Veto." Marketers have invested much time and effort in studying how to sidestep parents and teach kids how to get what they want. It is not surprising that the keynote address was given by none other than the marketing director of McDonald's, as a "softened parent veto" helps explain the 40 percent of fast food visits that occur due to requests and nagging by children. The strategy to bypass parents is a carefully calculated and deliberate business strategy. A former marketing employee states, "[It] was a conscious effort to move to direct kid marketing and not even worry about Mom. Just take her out of the equation." Marketers know that it is easy to take advantage of a parent's inability to say no to their child's buying requests because the "nag factor" is so strong. (5)

With approximately 30 percent of purchases resulting from the "nag factor," families are spending hundreds of dollars per month to appease the requests of their nagging children, turning these little consumers into big business. Companies cannot afford to leave this resource untapped. Millions of dollars have been invested into studying child behaviour and development in order to better understand the industry's target audiences. Companies employ psychologists, child development specialists, anthropologists, and sociologists to explore the drivers of children's anxieties and aspirations in a calculated and methodical manner. (2, 5) Researchers segment children by age (young, school age, tween), gender, income, geography, product usage, and lifestyle. (4) Individual children have even been identified among their peers as followers, influencers, or trend-setters. Thousands of children are interviewed each week so that companies remain "in the know" and are able to have an edge over their competitors regarding the latest childhood trends. (7)

The advertising industry has even identified various parenting styles, devising specific strategies to counteract each of them. In an influential "nag factor" study conducted in the mid-1990s, it was found that 70 percent of parents were receptive to child nagging. One-third of those parents were touted as indulgers or impulse buyers who readily succumbed to the children's requests. Fifteen percent were labelled as "kids' pals" who gave children significant choice regarding brand selection, while 20 percent were deemed "conflicteds," disliking child-focused advertising but finding it difficult to resist a child's requests. Only 13 percent were found to be unaffected by nagging, a group referred to as the "bare necessities" group. (5) As these statistics show, the family structure is being manipulated to encourage spending, with few families escaping the reach of this billion dollar business.

The harmful effects of child marketing on the family structure extend far beyond the financial sphere. Over the past few decades, North American parents have been spending less and less time with their children, largely owing to increased time spent in the workplace. Almost one-third of parents work these longer hours to pay for the non-essentials that their children have requested. (9) The irony here is that when polled, children overwhelmingly crave their parents' time and not their money. A 2003 poll asked 9 to 14-year-olds to name the one aspect of their parents' job that they would change. The majority, 63 percent, stated "more time to do fun things together." Of this 63 percent, 23 percent of children listed simple, inexpensive activities such as building a snowman or a tree house, going bike riding, or doing something outside as something they would like to do with their parents. Only 13 percent wished that their parents made more money. (5)

Marketers prey on the vulnerabilities of both children and parents. Market research has shown that "parents who spend less time with their children will spend more money on them." (5) Known as "guilt money," marketers have tapped into this wellspring of guilt and see it as an opportunity to increase profits and expand market share, with no concern about the resultant financial and family stresses. A vicious cycle ensues whereby increasing family consumption necessitates longer working hours, fuelling parental guilt. Attempting to compensate for less time spent with the family, more money is spent and the cycle continues.

It is likely that even the most savvy and informed parents are falling prey to the harmful effects of child marketing. Marketers have devised methods to target children outside of the watchful eyes of parents speaking directly to children in parent-free or anti-adult environments, including schools, television, and the Internet. (5) The 1980s saw an explosion of "kids only" media outlets, including television networks, radio stations, magazines, and clubs. (4) On August 1st, 1981, the first large-scale anti-adult environment was created when the first MTV music video was launched. As the first beats of "Video Killed the Radio Star" were aired, the eyes of marketers lit up. According to Juliet Schor, "MTV allowed teens to immerse themselves in an increasingly separate culture with its own fashions, language, and attitudes." (5)

Kids' own television programming has allowed marketing executives to sidestep media-savvy parents and put to use children's ability to influence their parents. (1) Studies continually show that increased television viewing is directly and positively correlated with increased purchase requests, generating a greater appetite for consumption. A Stanford Medical School study on third and fourth graders revealed that those whose television "viewing time declined made 70% fewer toy requests than those in the control group whose media habits were unchanged." (5) Clearly, then, an important action that parents can take to protect the family bank account, and, most important, the minds of their children, is to reduce their children's exposure to television and other forms of electronic media such as the Internet, radio, and video games. Given that two-thirds of children now have a television set in their bedrooms (many of them also have a computer as well), marketers have an increased ability to evade any form of parental supervision and thus directly persuade children and re-move any financially prudent messages such as frugality or debt avoidance. (2)

Critics and advertisers argue that parents always have the choice to turn off the family TV and computer to protect their children from the negative effects of advertising. However, in today's society, parents would need to turn off TV, movies, computers, radio, cell phones, and blindfold their children at the mall, school, and when they pass by the countless billboards hovering along our sidewalks and roads! In her book, *Can't Buy My Love*, Jean Kilbourne writes, "This is like telling us that we can protect our children from air pol-lution by making sure they never breathe." Even if parents could pro-tect their child from the media, they risk socially isolating their child from their peers. As "market-driven trends" play a larger role in struc-turing peer interactions, "parental restrictions put kids at risk of social exclusion."(5) Some media experts have gone so far as to argue "that the dominance of electronic media is so strong that prohibition de-prives children of basic cultural literacy." (5)

In addition to television and the Internet, schools provide the ideal parent-free zone to target children. Schools are the perfect arena for marketers who wish to promote products and corporate ideals without disruption or opposition. A Coca-Cola spokesperson relates the company's mandate as to "put soft drinks within arm's reach of desire." (3) Companies are training young consumers to give in to de-sire at a young and highly vulnerable age. For marketers, schools are ideal, as they provide a captive audience with no audience erosion with new "customers" walking through the door every year. Ed Win-ter of Channel One, a 12-minute news program designed for teens that is broadcast to schools across the United States, identifies the importance of school marketing: "Marketers have come to realize that all roads eventually lead to the schools." (2) According to Schor, the "commercial infiltration" of public schools has been the crown jewel for marketers, while in some cases, teachers have even been used as "brand ambassadors." (5)

Advertising in schools clearly violates the notion of "consumer sovereignty: the ability to escape ads and marketing." (5) Schools are intended to provide an environment that promotes learning and personal growth, not brand loyalty and the idea that spending more than you make is acceptable financial behaviour. As school is compulsory, it is fundamentally different from surfing the net, going to the mall, and watching MTV, making the presence of marketing to children and youth in these supposed "safe zones" all the more disturbing. Channel One is played in over 40 percent of U.S. middle and high schools. It is played on over 90 percent of school days and "is reported to be second only to the Super Bowl in audience size," promising advertisers "the undivided attention of millions of teenagers for 12 minutes a day." (2, 5, 7) The U.S. General Accounting Office frighteningly terms school marketing as "a growth industry." (2) If we are to develop healthy financial habits among our future generations, it is critical that our society re-evaluate the access that marketers are granted to schools.

"It takes a village to raise a child"

The oft-spoken old African proverb that it takes a village to raise a child speaks volumes to the need for community involvement in the development of children. To protect our children from the marketing industry, we must seek the support of others around us and join forces to try and counter the influence that this industry has over our children. The first step in addressing this problem is in recognizing that many parents are worried about the impact of marketing directed towards their children. When asked about child marketing, the vast majority of parents feel that "advertising and marketing aimed at kids has a negative effect" making them "too materialistic" and subjecting them to needless pressure "to buy things that are too expensive, unhealthy" and unnecessary. (5) Parents worry that their children learn to define self-worth with respect to what they own and the brands they wear, rather than based upon attributes such as thoughtfulness, caring, intelligence, and personality. (2, 5) Despite these concerns, even the most informed parents often feel paralyzed to act. The enduring battle for parents is in trying to find a healthy equilibrium between challenging an arsenal of child marketers, while simultaneously fostering societal integration, which is in itself a complex venture given the consumptive and economic nature of our society.

The development of a financially astute mind relies heavily on exposure to sound financial examples and truths, especially during one's formative years. Options other than consumption and debt must be introduced. Parents must serve as viable role models of responsible financial behaviour to ensure that appropriate ideals and practices are established. Teaching our children that thrift and frugality are to be respected and admired instead of frowned upon is an essential place to start. Unfortunately, the opposite often occurs, and misleading ideals such as greater income equals greater happiness and better brand equals better social status are instead propagated. Once these myths become entrenched in our belief system, they are not easily changed. As Harvard Professor Howard Gardner points out in his book, *Changing Minds*, once fundamental theories or ideas are engraved, they endure in our minds. When we then encounter ideas for which we are not prepared, or are in opposition to our previous "teachings," we revert to the original earlier engravings—in this case, spending and consuming. (10) If children continue to be exposed to our consumer culture and mass marketing at an early age, they will be unable to adapt to financially sound alternatives, such as simplicity and frugality.

When poor financial habits and skewed expectations about consumption are subconsciously ingrained into the minds of young people, they are often unable to cope responsibly when that first paycheque finally arrives. These young adults commonly rush out to buy what they have been convinced will provide fulfillment, with no consideration of the financial consequences. The desire and "need" for vehicles, homes, and vacations rise to the top of the priority list. Within a short time, they find themselves with 30-year mortgages, overwhelming vehicle expenses, lines of credit, credit cards, and no savings. A feeling of hopelessness develops and, with little to no financial resources, they avoid seeking financial advice. Even if financial advice is sought, advisors often find themselves in a difficult position. Financial recovery is largely dependant upon a client's willingness to live a different lifestyle, which many aren't willing to accept or aware of how to achieve. Moving from a reliance on credit towards saving 20 to 30 percent of one's gross income is a giant leap. The financial brainwashing and spending loyalty that occurred many years ago is exceedingly difficult to undo, but there is hope! Throughout the second part of the book, we will explore a number of ways in which parents can be positive financial role models for their children, apart from reducing exposure to electronic media and spending more time with their children.

The harmful financial and social effects of marketing directed towards children are extensive. Frequent child purchase requests and nagging significantly increase family spending, largely on "unnecessary" goods. Families are left with less disposable income for saving, with negative effects on both children and the family unit. Parents then succumb to longer work hours, with less time to spend with the family. The delayed and everlasting effects of child marketing are even more damaging. Children learn to base success and self-worth on "the perception of wealth," while the exposure to toxic spending, consumption, and branding habits during the formative years is nearly impossible to overcome. Adults then face an uphill battle when trying to restructure lifestyle patterns and expectations in an attempt to keep their heads above the financial waters.

As we have examined, our children play a pivotal role in our financial well-being. Whether it be through purchase requests, nagging, or guilt money, our children lead us to spend a significant share of the family budget on frivolous purchases. While I have already mentioned the benefits of turning off the TV and leading by example in order to help our children develop better financial habits, perhaps our best investment is simply to spend more time with our children. Studies repeatedly show that children most value their parents' time. Aside from the obvious benefits of developing a good relationship, by spending more time with our children in non-commercial environments, we will reduce nagging opportunities for new products. The more time we spend with our children, the more they will come to see our financial values.

Chapter 4

Spending to Belong and the New Necessities: The Second Assassin

Advertising's most important social function is to integrate the individual into our present-day American high-speed consumption economy.
—Pierre Martineau, former Research Director for the *Chicago Tribune*, 1957 (1)

We are hardwired to be manipulated by those retailers.
—Martin Lindstrom, quoted on NBC's *Today* show (2)

Advertising may be described as the science of arresting human intelligence long enough to get money from it.
—Stephen Leacock

The evolution of the consumer society and the role that marketers play makes them the most dangerous of the Money Assassins. Because companies and marketers have the most to lose, they have the greatest interest in keeping individuals consuming beyond their means and in debt. For consumer society to survive in its present form, it needs a mechanism that continually creates desires within the population to aspire to a standard of living that is perceived as better. If there are no reasons to consume, then the charade is up and it will be exposed for what it is: vanity and excess. Yet we must also recognize that we are also being exposed to the subtle yet extremely effective messages from the world of advertising. Consuming and marketing are not new, but having them as part of the fabric of daily life is, and this change has come at the cost of individuals' financial well-being. If we are to recapture our financial freedom, it is crucial that we make fundamental changes to our financial habits and respect the basic rule of spending less than we make. Although the marketing industry is constantly designing new ways to infiltrate and influence our thought processes, belief systems, and lifestyle aspirations, by bringing about awareness to consumptive communities, marketing tactics, the "new necessities," and our fears of social isolation, we can help protect ourselves from the financial hardships that are incurred by the pressures of spending to belong.

This chapter may seem somewhat out of context for a financial planning book, but if one hopes to eliminate debt and create wealth, getting to the root cause of our poor financial and spending habits is essential. As I mentioned in the introduction, getting to the root of our attitudes toward money is one of those surprising yet necessary topics that provides critical insights into our financial lives.

Many of us spend and consume to meet the requirements of our social, economic, and cultural communities. Much of this spending is done because our consumer society is accelerated by a continual competition for social standing. Similar to the role that we saw advertising play in the shaping of the financial mindset of our youth, the advertising and marketing industry is busy exploiting our insecurities and fears, helping to fuel a "new war of status competition and cultural consumption."(3) The ability of this industry to focus on our insecurities and fears has resulted in significant financial gains for corporations and substantial financial losses for a financially weakened population that cannot defend itself economically.

There has been a steady evolution in our consumer society where objects have adopted new layers of imagery. As a result of this evolution, both symbolism and meaning have come to be attached to goods, ultimately making the role goods play in our lives more complex and important. While goods were traditionally purchased and sold on the merits of their utility or usage, today many products and brands serve as "badges of group membership" communicating personal values, beliefs, and lifestyle preferences to others. The focus on products is now for them to "resonate with qualities desired by consumers...as social motivations for consumption." (3) The new role that products play in our lives is best described by the authors of *Social Communication in Advertising*:

> The product has become a totem, a representation of a clan or group that we recognize by its activities and its members' shared enjoyment of the product. The response to consumption seems to be less concerned with the nature of satisfaction than with its social meaning—the way it integrates the individual into a consumption tribe. Who is the person I become in the process of consumption? Who are the others like me? What does the product mean in terms of the type of person I am and how I relate to others? (3)

Consumptive Communities, Positional Goods, and Our Need to Belong

Who among us has never longed to belong to a group of people? As human beings, we are all wired to need the company of others. While some may consider themselves to be introverted, and others extroverted, the reality is that we are all inherently social beings. For this reason, we all make conscious or subconscious efforts to ensure that we are accepted into a group. While our need to belong to a group may manifest itself in joining a group of people with similar political views, religious views, academic interests, hobbies, interest in sports, etc., on some level we must make sacrifices to gain entry into the group. These sacrifices of sorts may come in the form of our time, energy, or money. While many of us may at times feel overwhelmed by our commitments to a group and the sacrifices made to maintain our "membership" in the group, today's biggest sacrifice is felt in our wallet. Simply put, we spend to belong.

The acts of consuming and spending are social experiences, so much so that both acts have come to serve as determinants of the communities we belong to. Although we often think of "our community" as the group of people who live in our neighbourhood, we also belong to a variety of other communities. If you define community as a sphere of people you interact with on a specific topic or interest, most of us belong to numerous communities. For example, the workplace, parenting circles, travel companions, fitness groups, places of worship, hobbies, sports, social circles, and volunteer organizations are examples of a few communities you may belong to. Although we do not always think of these associations as communities in the traditional sense, according to historian Daniel Boorstin, these communities play an important role in determining the health of our finances. Boorstin believes that we do not only look to our neighbourhoods to fulfill our sense of community but that we also observe the consumption behaviour of the individuals and groups we associate with in other areas of our life.

Throughout the 1960s and '70s, as our consumer society gained momentum, the patterns of consumer spending became a larger "force for social cohesion," and this social cohesion amongst groups of individuals gave rise to the term *consumption community*. (3) This term refers to the consumer or spending behaviour of individuals within a specific reference group. Many people value the relationships they have in their respective communities and therefore make an effort to ensure that they continue to belong to these groups. Many of us end up getting caught in the consumption trap, where we consume to maintain our standing within the group. While consumptive communities are not inherently good or bad, their influence on our financial well-being may be significant. It is very important that we be aware of the subtle expectations and pressures to consume that often go hand in hand with belonging to a specific community. This awareness is crucial, as the result of not paying heed to the pressures commonly associated with belonging to this type of community often leads us to spend beyond our means as well as spend out of line with our priorities and personal values. What often occurs is that we come to desire spending time with individuals in the group, and our actual purchases no longer serve as our raison d'être for being in the group in the first place. (3) While this desire is not in itself negative, the problem lies in the fact that the consumption community sets the baseline for acceptable or expected participation.

The concept of consumptive communities helps explain why a rise in our income does not necessarily guarantee higher levels of saving. As our incomes rise, we transition into new consumption communities. To belong to these new "communities," we often need to consume more than in our previous consumption community. Take, for example, someone who is promoted to upper management. Imagine the new expectations that might come with the position, ranging from what you wear, to where you eat, to where you live, to where you vacation, to what you drive. As we transition to new, more expensive "communities," the basics of life become more expensive and our income, both absolute and disposable, relative to our new peer group may actually feel like it is dropping. This phenomenon negates our raise to some extent, as we are now more financially constrained than before we took the new position.

Today's society is much more mobile than at any other time in history. We no longer limit our economic lives to exchanges undertaken face to face with local merchants, nor do we restrict our discussion about politics to local street corners. We live in a fundamentally different world than previous generations in that our values, feelings, and attitudes are no longer communicated through "everyday social interactions." (3) In today's fast-paced lifestyle, we often rely on shortcuts such as stereotypes and rules of thumb to help make sense of who and what is around us. Martin Lindstrom, author of *Buyology*, says that "85% of the time our brains are on autopilot" and that we rely on our unconscious minds to make our buying decisions because our conscious minds do not have the time. (4) To save time and ease this process, we put people, products, and services in neatly compartmentalized boxes. According to Robert Cialdini, author of *Influence*: "We cannot recognize and analyze all aspects of our lives and decisions…we don't have the time, energy or capacity" to fully evaluate and understand the actions of others. (5) Given the nature of our fast-paced lives and the accompanying time constraints we live with, we have learned to develop the ability to "fit in" quickly when entering new groups and social circles. There is no better proof of what is correct and acceptable than the actions of those around us. Cialdini refers to this form of evaluation as "social proof." Social proof is the method that we use to determine correct behaviour; it is the process whereby we determine what other people in the "community" deem to be correct and acceptable. An example of social proof in action is when you take up a new sport—golf, for example.

When we begin to golf, we want to fit in, so we observe and watch the etiquette and attire of seasoned golfers. Through this observation we quickly learn what is considered appropriate behaviour and what is not. Wanting to be accepted into our new-found community and demonstrate correct behaviour for this community—in this case, a community of golfers—we follow the principles of "social proof" and follow the actions of others in order to belong.

In the context of our discussion, this would refer to determining acceptable consumption behaviour. (5) Social proof assists us in identifying correct or acceptable consumer behaviour among our peers. Many of us want to know what others are doing before we decide to invest or purchase personal insurance. When faced with uncertainty, we look to others to guide our actions. (5) While this may sound like harmless behaviour, when we recognize that we also behave this way when we observe and emulate the spending habits of those around us, we begin to see the danger in modelling our spending habits according to what others are purchasing.

I believe there are two main reasons that explain the pervasive influence of social proof. First, no one wants to fall behind their peer group. We all want to be seen as "in the know" and trendy, and strive to keep pace with our neighbours to ensure that we maintain our share of the pie. The second reason can be described by the fact that there is safety in numbers. If everyone is acting in a similar fashion or purchasing the same products, there must be a good reason. No one wants to miss out or get left behind. If it turns out that everyone was wrong or duped, we can take comfort in knowing that we were not the only ones who lost. Misery loves company.

While many of us strive to be unique, the concepts of social proof and consumption communities have largely made us "all end up looking more or less predictably the same." (6) During the 1950s and '60s, some believed that the ability of many to buy washing machines, cars, and television sets was the beginning of the classless society and consumer democracy. There was widespread belief that everyone's standard of living would rise. This did not happen, as we neglected to consider the role that financial relativism plays in our lives. Instead of creating a consumer democracy of sorts, we have become financially enslaved and have been shaped to consume at the cost of our financial well-being out of fear that we might wake up and realize that we are "falling behind." (3)

The risk of falling behind or being social excluded or isolated from our peer group is a strong motivator for us to consume. Many of us constantly scan "the social landscape" to gage how we are doing compared to others, and more specifically, compared to those in our consumption communities. (3) Much of this fear is fuelled by the fast-paced tempo of technology that serves to constantly bombard us with messages about new ways of communicating and more efficient ways of working and completing tasks. We are surrounded by people who keep intense work paces and believe it when we hear that "time is money." In watching these people work faster than we do and getting more work done, we assume that they must be making more money or will move up the corporate ladder sooner than we will. Simply put, we are left feeling that we will be left behind or overlooked.

Throughout the course of our lives, we have all felt at one time or another as if our consumption behaviour were being scrutinized, evaluated, or judged. We may have felt scrutinized or judged by driving a second-hand car, wearing the wrong clothes, living in the wrong neighbourhood, or being viewed as cheap. When we feel this way, we are essentially experiencing a kind of performance anxiety where we fear being exposed or deemed inadequate. From a psychological perspective, the authors of *Reinventing Your Life*, Jeffrey Young and Janet Klosko, refer to this fear as the "social exclusion lifetrap." Everyone's sensitivity to being judged is different; some march to their own tune, while others follow close behind. Our fear of not belonging to a desired "community" becomes a key element in adopting new lifestyle or consumption practices. (3) As we will see later in this chapter, it is predicted that companies will increase the intensity and pressure on exploiting our personal fears and insecurities in order to take advantage of the feeling that, without the company's product or service, we are missing out or being left behind. (4) Many of us have been driven to adopt unsustainable and dangerous financial behaviours as a result of our deep-seated fears of not belonging to a desired group.

Let's look at an example of the social pressure to consume. You decide that you want to reduce your debt and realize that you spend a lot of money on eating out. By making the financially prudent decision to cut back on this expenditure, you have had to decline a few invites to dine out with friends and acquaintances. How many times can you decline these invites until your friends stop inviting you out? Your friends may be completely unaware of your goal to reduce debt, and because you feel embarrassed or believe that discussing money is taboo, you never explain why it is that you no longer join them to go out. According to one survey, Canadians are more comfortable discussing their love life, religion, and politics than they are discussing their personal finances. (7) While some people may confide in a close friend, most people would not discuss their financial troubles with others who are outside of their inner circle.

Take another example. You have a group of friends who go on a trip together every year. The trips began as long weekends to the mountains or local resorts when everyone was in school or beginning their careers. However, as everyone's income rose, the trips became week-long excursions to Mexico and Cuba. While you may still be able to afford the trip, you would rather use this money for other priorities in your life, such as a down payment for a home or a financial safety net. Ultimately, though, you decide to go, as you value these friendships and want to spend time with your friends, even if it means spending beyond your means.

The above example is not meant to try and dissuade you from ever going on another trip, as this is not the message I am trying to put across. Rather this example serves to remind us of the thousands of dollars that are spent on our social desire to belong. In most cases, spending to belong is not about affordability but rather about priorities. In the hierarchy of needs, after food, shelter, and water are provided, humans desire to belong and be loved—a fundamental need that should not cost us our financial well-being. Unfortunately, many people feel the need to spend their money to satisfy the need to belong, and, as a result, their financial well-being takes a back seat.

In his 1976 book, *Social Limits to Growth*, Fred Hirsch coined the term *positional goods*. The term refers to goods that can easily, quickly, and visibly communicate or imply social status, standing, or position. Since the 1970s, the increased prominence of positional goods in our lives has had a significant impact on our financial behaviour, specifically our spending habits. Positional goods are generally exclusive and scarce, such as beach or waterfront property, antiques, desirable neighbourhoods, limited edition vehicles, and VIP services. Unlike regular goods that can be mass-produced to meet demand, the production of positional goods is limited and in short supply. (8) As affluent consumers purchase top-of-the-line positional goods, the rest of us are forced to consume more regular goods just to maintain our relative social position. Yet as the overall wealth, or at least our access to cash (otherwise, in many cases, known as debt) rises, the proportion of positional goods in circulation becomes larger. Affluent consumption communities are largely responsible for creating positional goods because a positional good is only desirable if others, usually in the upper classes, desire these goods. These goods often play a pivotal role in creating a competition for social standing. This competition leads to an environment of competitive consumption, where we try and "out-consume" each other to maintain our current position. (3) In fact, consumption has even become defensive in nature, as many of us "spend to avoid falling behind."

To understand the reasons why many of us consume for status, we must look at the idea of the massification of products. The massification of goods or products simply means goods that were once affordable only to the wealthy becoming more affordable to the larger population due to mass production of the goods, resulting in lower prices—just think of computers as a good example. Or look in the not too distant past when owning a television was somewhat of a luxury, driving a car implied wealth, and travelling abroad was reserved for the rich! This past bears little resemblance to the present, where most stratas of society can afford TVs, vehicles, and holidays without being considered well off. Yet this massification of products, whereby the masses of people now have access to products that were once reserved for the elite, has had a profound impact on our financial well-being. Now that the majority can afford a new baseline of consumption, higher ranks of society seek new levels of consumption, such as flying first class or belonging to preferred customer programs with preferential and exclusive treatment. Now that other classes of society can have a taste of the "high life," largely through debt, "elites" have had to use these new ways of distinguishing themselves. The financial cost of trying to keep up with more expensive styles of living is obvious: higher levels of debt. The consequence of today's escalation of spending expectations has made many individuals slaves to competitive consumption. (3)

If we buy into this mentality of goods and spending as determinants of social rank, we will be caught in a never-ending cycle of spending beyond our means to maintain social position. Being aware of or uncovering our unconscious motive for consumption can break the cycle and explain much of our unconscious, competitive consumption and spending. Consumption communities, financial invisibility, positional goods, and the fear of falling behind all contribute to our larger need to "spend to belong." There are some who will reject the need to spend to belong, but for the vast majority, this need is so pervasive and unobserved that even the most astute, disciplined, smart, and informed individuals are subject to this new financial threat. "Spending to belong" bears a financial cost second to none and also has significant non-financial costs such as longer work days, less time with family, less satisfaction with consumption, and environmental waste. Thousands of dollars are at stake, and the battle between individuals and marketers is on. Currently, the marketers are winning. That is where we will turn our attention to so that we can discover why they are winning and how we can stop them.

The Consumer Matrix

Advertising helps to keep the masses dissatisfied with their mode of life, discontented with ugly things around them. Satisfied customers are not as profitable as discontented ones.
—Trade journal, *Printer's Ink*, from the 1930s (3)

It is often believed that the lies we are told are the killers of truth. But it turns out, at least in finance, the myths that go unchallenged and mistakenly form part of our belief system are the most harmful.

In today's consumer society, there is no greater myth than the belief that our daily decisions in regards to both our personal and financial lives are not influenced by marketing and advertising. Many people enjoy advertisements and see them as harmless, playful, innocent, and fun. Some even view them as a form of art. Throughout my life, I have laughed at and enjoyed many commercials myself. I am not disputing the entertainment value of commercials, but only highlighting that, for the purpose of breaking free of debt, spending less than we make, and discovering a life a financial well-being, it is critical that we understand how and in what ways marketing and advertising have evolved to take a new and damaging role in our lives. Since the 1970s and '80s, marketing and advertising have quietly undergone a transformation elevating consumption from a functional or utility perspective to a social process that has become one of the main communicators of personal status, lifestyle, wealth, and meaning.

According to the authors of *Social Communication in Advertising,* "consumption is meant to be a spectacle," as it is an experience and a way of life. The authors use the analogy of theatre to describe the spectacle of consumption. They ask us to think of marketers as the hosts of the event and advertisers as the master of ceremonies or composers whose job it is to ensure an ample supply of new and entertaining products are regularly displayed, creating "imaginary appetites" in the stomachs and minds of theatregoers. (1) The stage of consumption is often brilliant, tantalizing, and enticing to such an extent that it can distract theatregoers from other important values and goals in life, such as financial prudence. Consumers have become enraptured by the performance that has been put on display. (3)

Another way that consumption has evolved to influence our feelings of belonging can be seen in the commonalities consumption has with religion. Martin Lindstrom, a leading marketing expert, discovered that products and brands had a lot in common with religion and rituals. Lindstrom believes that there are ten common pillars in every leading religion: "a sense of belonging, a clear vision, power over enemies, sensory appeal, storytelling, grandeur, evangelism, symbols, mystery and rituals." (4) The reasons why this connection between religion and consumption is important is that as our lives have become more frantic and unsettled, individuals naturally look for stability and familiarity. Advertisers have been able to create similar experiences and feelings with brands and products, giving, as Lindstrom writes, "an illusion of comfort and belonging." (4) Because of the power and attractiveness of these qualities, consumption, and the product and services that come along with it, have evolved to take on a new place and priority in our lives.

Now that advertising is "fully integrated into our cultural repertoire" we accept and tolerate it as part of our daily lives. (3) One aspect that differentiates today's "society from earlier ones is not only the sheer volume of goods and services available to consumers…but also the sheer intensity of the promotional effort." (3) Every day, North America's subconscious is exposed to billions of advertisements and commercials through a variety of media such as billboards, radio, television, movies, video games, and the Internet. Unfortunately, our culture has become saturated with messages telling us to consume, forming part of our cultural landscape. Everywhere we look, we find ourselves as active participants in the consumer society performance; it surrounds us and we cannot escape it. One of the reasons for the pure volume and intensity of advertising is that our conscious mind only registers 8 percent of an ad's message. Rance Crain of *Advertising Age* says that after our brains take in the initial message, "the rest is worked and reworked deep within the recess of the brain, where a product's position and reposition take shape." (10) The overall incessant message is that in some ways our lives are not exciting enough. We are all vulnerable on some level, and marketers find a way to attack our inadequacies, insecurities, and guilt, while exploiting our fears, greed, and envy. (11, 12) Those who work in the marketing and advertising industry are surely not evil and are simply doing their job. Unfortunately, a job well done in their industry can have severe consequences that can be destructive to the financial prosperity of many.

All advertising to some degree suggests that the purchase of a product or service will lead to a more exciting and fulfilling life or satisfy any feelings of insecurity or inadequacy that we might have. If there were only a few advertisements telling these stories, there would likely not be a problem. However, as we are bombarded on a daily basis, the sheer volume and intensity make even the most astute individuals vulnerable. Over time, we all become vulnerable to the message that these proposed ways of living and consuming must be expected and normal. Our daily consumption perspectives and judgments become skewed, numbed, and uncritical, allowing our money to be spent on someone else's priorities and not on our own personal and family values.

Traditionally, advertisers tried to convince consumers to buy their products by using a rational approach, appealing to the usefulness and utility of the product. It was during the 1930s and '40s that symbolism and personal use became the focus of ads and the consumer society was born. Today, instant gratification, personalized products, the buying experience, and capturing the consumer's soul are the focus of marketing efforts. Playing a more personal and transformational role, marketers try to alter consumer attitudes toward lifestyle and social success, making products a vehicle for social utility as opposed to product functionality. (3) The nature of this transformation has been rooted in the change in the social function of goods. Traditionally, goods were primarily seen as satisfiers of wants. Yet over time, and as a result of much effort and a changing role of marketing, products were released from the constraints of utility and came to be cloaked in layers of imagery and symbolism. Today, ads are viewed as natural means of communicating happiness, meaning, and social success. (3) Companies know and understand that their businesses success, whether it be in computers or clothing, depends upon creating and producing powerful images and brands that connect with individuals. The pressure to communicate our values and meaning through consumerism has reached such a point that we have unknowingly accepted financial enslavement as the cost and the consumer matrix as our environment.

It is hard to find an industry that argues its ineffectiveness and speaks in such a self-deprecating fashion as the advertising and marketing industry. Companies, especially in the alcohol and tobacco industry, employ multi-billion-dollar advertising campaigns and then turn around and deny that advertising and marketing have any effect on consumers and their choices. (10) The marketing industry argues that their efforts are to persuade and inform consumers, to only "shift brand preferences within product sectors," not to manipulate individuals. (3) Some in the advertising industry claim that advertisers simply respond and adapt to what consumers want. However, others, such as Rance Crain, argue that advertising "plays the tune," suggesting that they set the agenda "rather than just dancing to the tune." (10) Marketing expert Martin Lindstrom believes we have been "hardwired to be manipulated." It is the job of the advertising world to make sure individuals crave products as well as create a constant desire for a new, "improved," and "progressive" lifestyle. Overall, marketing and advertising efforts are deceptive in that their underlying subtle message, that without their product or service our life is in some way inadequate, is untrue and misleading. If it were just one ad that was being repositioned and shaped into our minds, it would not be a big deal. But with every company that has something to sell pressuring and influencing us, the pressure and influence to spend has had a cumulative effect on a nation in debt, where spending beyond our means is out of control. In short, advertising suggests consumerism is the only path to achieve personal pleasure and social success. Unfortunately, these notions are often myths and lies that come at significant costs to our personal time, energy, family, environment, and bank accounts.

Consumer "Free Choice"?

The basis for many of marketers' commercial strategies has emerged from the field of human psychology. The key component of human psychology that serves to assist marketers in their mission is found in the general theory that the consumer psyche is ruled by irrational insecurities. (3) The advertising industry has long believed that irrationality is at the heart of consumption and that the illusion of consumer "free choice" is vital to the success of consumer society. Economists would like us to believe that we have full "consumer sovereignty" and act with "rational, free choice," but today's consumer culture significantly hinders free choice, especially when it comes to our spending habits. The social pressure to participate in and belong to our respective consumptive communities is significant. For the illusion of free choice to work, individuals must believe that their consumer choices are free from any outside influences, as many of us erroneously do believe. (13) The majority of Canadians believe that advertising plays a greater role in influencing society than schools, yet also believe that advertising does not influence consumer choices. (3) The belief that advertising and marketing influences society while somehow eluding us on an individual level comes as no surprise, as none of us want to believe that we are being taken, duped, or manipulated. Most of us consider ourselves to be smart enough not to get lured in. The same belief structure is at play when 70 percent of respondents describe "the average American" as "very materialistic," while only 8 percent feel they are materialistic themselves. (6) The problem is that if everyone else is being influenced and we follow the principles of social proof, watching the behaviours of others and then following them, then in fact we are also being influenced. This is the perfect scenario for marketers to be the most effective; individuals believe that they have not been influenced while in reality they have been exposed to the most significant and effective type of persuasion: the actions and behaviour of others.

Man has been called the reasoning animal, but he could with greater truthfulness be called the creature of suggestion.
—Leiss et al. *Social Communication In Advertising*

No matter how pure a rational decision may seem, it has been deeply influenced by emotional forces, conscious or unconscious. It turns out that our actions are more like a "conditioned reflex" to prompts and suggestions than based on rational thoughts. (5) As we will explore shortly, the real reason behind many of our consumer purchases, which occur at an unconscious level, lies in the fact that our decision-making process, burdened with a gluttony of consumer choices and information overload, has had to become more automated to survive. Marketing experts believe that when their arsenal of marketing tactics are unleashed to influence individuals to consume, the "rational mind doesn't stand a chance." (4) Therefore, while on the one hand individuals are making the rational choice to spend and consume to belong, fulfilling one of our most basic physiological needs, on the other hand we are making the very irrational decision to sacrifice our financial well-being and security. Harvard Professor David Laibson says, "Our emotional brain wants to max out the credit card, even though our logical brain knows we should save for retirement." (4) Marketers know this and exploit our emotional and irrational decision-making process at the cost of our financial security.

The idea that we have freedom of choice in our decision-making process has been confused with our real desire for liberty. Liberty is "the availability of opportunities to be the author of your life and to make it meaningful and significant." (14) Freedom of choice is limited to making choices within the constraints and confines of our consumer society. We should be in search of liberty of choice, to be the author of our lives, not freedom of choice, which restricts us only to the options presented to us by marketers and advertisers. It is our attachment to a materialistic lifestyle that gives us the illusion of freedom of choice within the context of consumer society, but the consumer matrix fails to give us the freedom to choose the life we truly desire. The attachment to this belief keeps us trapped within the walls of our consumer society and the financial consequences that come along with it.

Marketing Research, Technology, and Science

In the early years of marketing, marketers required a greater psychological understanding of individuals to build stronger relationships and connections between the individual and the objects to be purchased. To facilitate this greater understanding, companies and marketers needed an environment "where the meaning of things [could] resonate in response to an individual's changing emotional states." (3) Today's consumer culture is the result of over 50 years of social research, which has unified and served business, advertising, and the mass media as a way to influence and develop today's culture. The goal of advertising and marketing research is "to understand how consumers experience the meaning of products and how they formulate the intention to purchase." (3) This information is then used to construct campaigns that connect with the inner desires of consumers.

Economist John Kenneth Galbraith emphasized "producers of conspicuous goods do not merely inform us of the merits of their products. They also attempt to persuade us to believe we need them, using all the tools in the modern social psychologist's arsenal." (15) With this observation, the stage was set for objects to become the main attraction in many of our lives with the birth of marketers' ability to access and explore the innermost recesses of individuals' thinking and emotions. It was during the 1960s that agencies began accessing data that would assist them in transforming and reorienting the practice of advertising into a science that could tap into and exploit people's insecurities, delusions, and attachments. (3) Motivational research borrowed a premise from Freudian psychology that holds that our real motives are hidden and that to discover our insecurities and anxieties, research would have to extract this information through non-threatening means. (3) Today, much of this information is extracted from us without our knowledge or consent. Just think of how many times your personal information and purchasing patterns have been tracked, studied, and sold.

Advancements in technology have allowed marketers to gain a greater understanding of our consumptive habits in an extremely rapid time. Almost every time you swipe a rewards or points or credit card, the time, place, amount, and item purchased is being tracked and analyzed in the hope of discovering new information about you and how to persuade you to consume and spend more. This process is called data mining and it is big business. In *Why We Buy*, author Paco Underhill talks about how businesses use "trackers." Trackers are hired to stealthily follow shoppers and note everything they do while in the store. Analyzing shopping has become a science that assesses 900 aspects of shopper-store interactions. Marketers want to know and understand the full experience of the consumer, including how they enter a store, how they navigate it, how they handle the merchandise, how they interact with display ads, and how long their shopping experience lasts. All of this information that is being gathered, recorded, and tracked is ultimately used to increase sales and revenue in order to secure increased spending for the consumer. (16) Not only is the job of advertising and marketing researchers to monitor consumer behaviour, but it is to immerse themselves into the consumers' world "until the point of view of the consumer permeates the planner's thinking." (3) This immersion leads to the discovery of critical insights upon which the marketing team can build a powerful campaign.

Technology is also developing new ways to reach consumers. For example, it is likely that in the near future advertisers will be able to play different commercials in homes targeted at varying demographics. A commercial that promotes a vacation getaway to the Bahamas will be tailored for viewers who are watching the same show. If you were watching your favourite show and were between the ages of 40 and 55, had kids, and earned $100,000, you would receive a different commercial than your neighbour who is between 25 and 35, has no kids, and earns $50,000. Technology is making advertisers more efficient in their ability to tailor commercials to appeal to specific consumptive communities. These technological advancements have resulted in increased efficiency and profit for companies at the cost of exposing and taking advantage of consumers' vulnerabilities.

But the ultimate goal for market research has always been to actually get into the minds of consumers, specifically the unconscious mind, where over 90 percent of purchasing decisions are thought to occur. (4) Martin Lindstrom, author of *Buyology*, writes that the key to unlocking consumer's subconscious thoughts, and discovering the desires and feelings that drive those thoughts, can be found in the science of neuromarketing. Neuromarketing at its core is the controversial science of watching and measuring brain activity to allow companies to enhance the effectiveness of connecting their product, brand, and message with the subconscious thoughts of the consumer mind. According to Lindstrom, neuromarketing reveals how branding and other marketing tactics work on the human brain, how individuals react to different types of stimuli, and how our unconscious minds control our behaviour and feelings. It is the hope of some marketers that neuromarketing will significantly assist them in identifying the "craving spot" of consumers in hopes of encouraging individuals to continually buy more. Lindstrom speculates that there will be an increase in our national obsession with consumption as marketers become more effective at exploiting our subconscious desires. (4)

What market researchers know is that our decisions to buy are built over a lifetime of product associations. Our brains rely on these past associations as shortcuts to make purchasing decisions. Martin Lindstrom calls these associations "bookmarks of the brain." (4) The technical term for these "bookmarks" is *somatic markers*. Many of our past associations are commonly part of what is called "sensory branding." This type of branding not only focuses on the visual aspect of a product but also on the feel, smell, and sound of the product by fully engulfing an individual and preparing them to be triggered to buy sometime in the future. Two examples of this subtle covert marketing include when Gordon's gin experimented with filling British movie theatres with the scent of juniper berries to remind moviegoers of the taste of gin. Another example would be when Calvin Klein stuck CK Be perfume strips on the back of Ticketmaster concert envelopes. (17) Lindstrom says that some of the most powerful somatic markers are rooted in fear and advertisers are "all too happy to take advantage of our stressed out, insecure, increasingly vulnerable natures." (4)

Yet for marketing to be efficient, it does not always need to rely on technology. For power and influence to be effective, it must remain invisible. Marketers have devised a method that enables them to go about their work unnoticed by blending into a crowd. The cutting edge strategy of undercover marketing is to perpetuate the illusion of "free consumer choice," where success necessitates the deceiving of consumers. Here's how it works. "Operatives," or hired salespeople, enter your daily routine and begin talking about and using products and services that they have been hired to promote. In essence they are using and exploiting the power of social proof. Jonathan Ressler, marketing visionary and founder of Big Fat Promotions in New York, says that individuals are constantly being marketed to without them ever knowing it. "It happens in bars, it happens at soccer games, it happens in shopping malls, it happens in subways...so there's stuff going on all around you all the time—which

I know is kind of scary." (18)

What this all means to one's financial well-being is that the financial mind is under a tremendous assault. The financial consequence of this sensory assault is that it has been and will continue to be extremely difficult to spend less than one makes. In many ways, marketers know us better than we know ourselves, though they will not admit it and we will not allow ourselves to believe it. This, though, is exactly the way the marketing and advertising industry wants it. Limiting one's exposure to marketing has become impossible, unless individuals begin to refuse to accept an economy that is designed and dependant upon the slight-handed tactics of marketers and advertisers. Individuals must counter this persuasion and protect their money by reducing their exposure to the marketing industry, being aware of the industry's presence at all times, and being clear about their own personal priorities and goals to avoid being tempted to go off track. Marketing and advertising have immense power and influence over our financial psyche. As our mind is our most powerful tool in eliminating debt, creating wealth, and empowering consumer sovereignty, it is obvious that vigilance is needed in protecting our financial mindset at all costs.

TV and Product Placements

> *TV will never be a serious competitor for radio because people must sit and keep their eyes glued on a screen; the average American family hasn't time for it.*
> —Author unknown, from the *New York Times*, 1939

The introduction of commercial television in the 1950s launched the "quintessential communications form of the modern era." (3) The tie between TV and consumerism began with the development of soap operas in the 1930s, with the goal of developing product "tie-ins." (3) The lines between entertainment and advertising have, in many cases, become indistinguishable. Television, magazine, and radio organizations are dependent upon marketing expenditures for billions of dollars of revenue. According to one ABC executive, "The network is paying affiliates to carry network commercials, not programs. What we are is a distribution system for Proctor & Gamble." (10)

During the mid-1960s, program sponsors wanted to encourage viewers to yearn for a more glamorous, consumer-oriented lifestyle. As a result, numerous prime-time hit shows such as *The Beverly Hillbillies* and *The Andy Griffith Show* were dropped because they attracted elderly, low-income, and rural viewers—the wrong type of audience for sponsors. (3) Today, advertising is not limited to commercials, as programs themselves agree to advertise products during the episodes. Characters in the hit show *Dawson's Creek* not only all wore J.Crew clothing, the set of the show itself resembled a J.Crew catalogue, and characters in the show even mentioned J.Crew. (17) The explosion of product placements can be traced back to 1982 with a little Reese's Pieces–eating alien, E.T. (9) Today, movies such as *Space Jam* have taken sponsors and have made them the movie. "Michael, it's showtime. Get your Hanes on, lace up your Nikes, grab your Wheaties and Gatorade, and we'll pick up a Big Mac on the way!" Obviously, sponsor McDonald's supplied the toys and Happy Meals. (17) While marketing in children's TV and movies is more obvious, the type of marketing that occurs in adult programs is more subtle in order to meet the requirement of silent persuasion. That said, the next time you watch an episode of *24*, you won't need to look hard to find a product placement for the automotive industry in the middle of your screen. But there has always been a debate about the effectiveness of subliminal advertising and about whether or not it really works. Well, marketing guru Martin Lindstrom wanted to find the answer, and after much research his answer was, "yes—chillingly well." (4) What this means to our financial beliefs and subconscious mind is that it will continue to be under attack, with little to no help or protection.

Forget Keeping Up with the Joneses, It's the Jetson's You Should Be Worried About!

The phrase "Keeping up with the Joneses" dates back to an early 1900s cartoon and refers to trying to keep up with the material possessions of one's neighbours. We all want a sense of our financial situation vis-à-vis our peers. The advertising industry has been kind enough to provide a never-ending array of possible comparisons, standards, and judgments. As we explored earlier, the notion of relative or perceived social and class position is the lead driver in many of our behaviours and purchasing decisions. We all claim that we are not concerned about keeping up with others, yet our actions, spending habits, and accumulation of debt tell a different story. Our goal now is not solely to keep up with our neighbours but rather to keep pace with the idea or notion of what constitutes "the good life," a notion that has been communicated through mass media. We are attempting to keep up with people who we do not know, who we will never meet, and who are living lives that are false, unrealistic, and financially rare.

I believe that we have transitioned from "keeping up with the Joneses" to keeping up with a futuristic or fictitious family we do not even know, like "The Jetsons" from the 1960s cartoon. "Keeping up with the Jetsons" is more dangerous than the Joneses, as it is an endless universe of consumer expectations that spans an array of cultural and financial backgrounds and opportunities. One of the largest differences between the Joneses and the Jetsons is that the Joneses, your neighbours, are real, while the Jetsons can be the make-believe creation of some product or television executive. If possessions and consumption establish status, then the criteria for success is forever changing, as can be seen when you flip the channel and get a whole new set of standards to measure up to. Your neighbour is more static and concrete. With your neighbour, "what you see is what you get." The Jetsons, on the other hand, constantly change, move, upgrade, and keep a pace that is impossible to keep up with. (3) In our attempt to keep up, we sacrifice the real wealth in our lives that can be found in our leisure time, love, friendship, and health, all while being mislead by false promises.

The New Necessities

When we have provided against cold, hunger and thirst, all the rest is but vanity and excess.
—Seneca (19)

There has been a profound change in our society in terms of the way we express ourselves. Our purchased goods have become extensions or expressions of who we are and who we want to be. A part of our soul can now be found in our vehicles, home entertainment systems, appliances, cell phones, and clothing. Our newfound yearning to satisfy individual wants and address personal satisfaction has blurred the distinction between real needs and desires, costing some their financial freedom. (20) Over one-third of Americans earning between $50,000 and $100,000 a year say that they spend nearly all their income on the basic necessities of life. More shocking still is that nearly 20 percent of those who earn more than $100,000 say the same thing. (6) For centuries, food, shelter, and clothing were considered to be the basic necessities of life. However, as our consumer society has evolved, consumers are no longer clear about what constitutes a "necessity."

In taking a closer look, we discover that many individuals are wasting much of their hard-earned and valuable money on the "new necessities." The "necessities" of life have quickly evolved. This evolution largely explains why we have such high levels of personal debt, as well as a general inability to save. Wealth and progress are no longer found in comfort, but rather in pleasure. In our pursuit for pleasure, we find ourselves caught in a constant cycle. Goods that began as pleasurable eventually come to be recognized as goods that provide us with comfort. As a result, we continue to spend more in order to rediscover our original feeling of pleasure, and the cycle of needing "new necessities" continues. (14) Developing an awareness of the "new necessities" is a precursor to making positive financial change, creating wealth, eliminating debt, and simplifying our lives, but we are unwilling to cut back on luxury items that we now consider essentials. This unwillingness to change is the result of the fact that "we are caught both in social and economic conditions that keep us participating in the system." (6)

The constant production of new goods has created inequalities that have fuelled "status wars which create a continual expansion of needs as people attempt to distinguish themselves from each other." (3) This has provided the marketing industry and many businesses with the opportunity to shape the social agenda and define what is considered a necessity or luxury. The outcome of this transformation has resulted in an increased number of people who are compelled to spend beyond their means to keep up with others and maintain their social standing. The financial consequence of this new phenomenon is a life burdened by debt.

As we explored in a previous chapter, studies reveal that once a basic level of shelter, food, and clothing has been attained, our level of happiness does not increase as additional material wealth is consumed. Yet the notion of what constitutes a "basic" level has been shifting and is increasingly harder to define. For example, dishwashers, air conditioning, computers, cell phones, gift spending, microwave ovens, home entertainment systems, exotic vacations, and multiple vehicle ownership were once considered frivolous and excessive in the eyes of past generations. In the eyes of most of us today, these goods are now regarded as a necessary part of daily life. The "new necessities" have penetrated all corners of our lives and in the process they have redefined our basic consumption standards and expectations. We now have much higher expectations regarding our home, family, work, vehicle, vacations, weddings, and even pets. An important aspect of these "new necessities" is the way in which our expectations regarding necessity and success have been altered. When new products enter the marketplace, our standards of consumption are reset and reframed, increasing the financial costs of our "baseline of needs" and making it much more difficult to satisfy our needs. Although we can take part and enjoy these new products and services within the guidelines of financial prudence, we must also evaluate their usefulness and question how and where they fit into our priority list. As the environmental and financial costs associated with the new necessities are very high, we must seriously consider the role they play in our lives before we simply jump on board.

The arrival of new products and services in the marketplace is not a new phenomenon. It is rather the incredible speed at which these new products arrive and their ability to penetrate the pocketbooks that has changed. Take weddings, for example. Wedding proposals did not always begin with a diamond engagement ring. It was only 50 years ago that a faltering diamond industry was bolstered by the hugely successful "A Diamond is Forever" campaign. Engagement rings have become a norm in today's engagements, and those proposing are now expected to spend two months of their salary when buying a ring. There is no economic or financial reasoning for this suggestion other than it sets a precedent for what is "acceptable" and normal. (13) While MasterCard might remind us of the many things that are priceless in life, there is a clear price associated with getting married. Although I would never try to discourage anyone from trying to make their wedding day as memorable and enjoyable as possible, I am concerned by the financial strain that the $25,000 cost of an average wedding places on newlyweds.

Technology and communication devices, with their planned obsolescence that require us to upgrade on a regular basis, are formidable expenses that we did not have to incur in the past in order to belong. Twenty years ago, you were set if you had a phone with a land line, cable, VCR, and maybe a VIC-20 or Commodore 64. Today's "necessities" might include cable or satellite, HDTV, DVD (maybe Blu-ray), a digital camera, a cell phone for everyone in the family, Bluetooth devices, a desktop computer, a couple of laptops, a wireless web connection, a variety of adapters and chargers, not to mention the Nintendo DS, Playstation, and video screens in the back of the head rests in the vehicle. As I said before, while technology has brought much enjoyment and leisure into our lives, it has had a much different effect on our financial well-being.

Part of what fuels our consumer society and keeps us in debt is the significant amount of money that we spend on gifts. (6) Whether it is a gift for a birthday, a wedding, Christmas, a baby shower, a pet, or graduation, gifting norms and costs have risen and captured a greater portion of everyone's wallet. The commercialization of gifting is accompanied by significant social pressures and expectations. We all want to be seen as thoughtful, considerate, and caring, and gifts are one way to express our sincerity. Yet with one-third of us unable to remember what we gave our significant other last year for Christmas, our heartfelt giving may not be exactly what it appears to be. (1) Christmas was once the only time of year that retailer's had seasonal commercialism. Today, the giving season never ends, with New Year's, Valentine's Day, St. Patrick's Day, Easter, Mother's and Father's Day, national holiday celebrations, wedding anniversaries, work anniversaries, birthdays, graduations, Thanksgiving, Halloween, and many other occasions to buy gifts for others. There are less expensive alternatives to showing that we are creative, that we care, and that we are thoughtful, such as giving our time and energy, yet our personal time is already constrained. Also, for many the social risk of these alternatives being interpreted as cheap or thoughtless is too great, so it is both easier and safer to buy our belonging and acceptance. The total financial cost of gifting is unknown, but given that Christmas bills take, on average, six months to pay off, one might guess that the figure would be surprisingly high. (21)

One of the most notable areas infiltrated by the "new necessities" involves our children. Sadly, recent surveys show that more parents describe children as "expensive" than "enjoyable." (13) With baby strollers ranging from $200 to $1,000, car seats up to $400, and baby carriers up to $200, just the investment required to carry one's children around is a small fortune. Now consider toys, accessories, activities, education, lessons, child care, and clothing, and we quickly see how the line between "need" and "desire" becomes blurry when it comes to our expenditures on our children. Next time you go shopping in a children's store, note how many outfits cost more than what you would find in an adult store, regardless of the fact that your child will grow out of the outfit by the time you get home! Although shopping and spending on our children can be a lot of fun, we must exercise some degree of caution and use our common sense or risk seriously damaging the family's finances while transferring poor financial habits to our children.

There are many other examples of the "new necessities" that

pressure us to increase our spending, such as vacations, transportation, hobbies, entertainment and pets, to list a few. In addition to the pressure to spend out of "necessity," all of the "new necessities" have their own consumptive communities, adding another level of pressure. Ultimately, what is important to note and be aware of is the increased social pressure to spend and to question whether what others consume are really necessities.

Solutions!

Our value system must change so that we have everything that we need without needing everything we see.
—Ivan Hoffman, *The Tao of Money*

If you buy-in to enough of these false realities, you get duped into believing that you are focusing on success.
—Vincent M. Roazzi, *The Spirituality of Success: Getting Rich with Integrity*

The desire and pressures to consume the "new necessities" and to "spend to belong" exists in us all. While some people are aware of these pressures and are able to suppress any desires, others are unaware of their own need to play the game. The pressure to spend has risen rapidly in recent years. Year after year, the "new necessities" have grown exponentially and have reached a point where their collective impact has eroded our ability to save. Our financial psyche is now programmed to believe that there is a perceived value or necessity in the "new necessities." As a result, we must devote a larger share of our energy and income to pay for them. (3) A layering effect of new expenses has occurred, and will be passed on, along with the financial burden, from generation to generation.

Many of us sense that something is wrong with our economic model but find it difficult to pinpoint the problem. Our inability to locate this problem stems from the fact that we have been transformed over time into developing new financial habits and buying into the falsehood of material progress. In many regards, we have used our advances and progress for convenience, vanity, and self-indulgence instead of for a greater purpose. For example, in 1973 only 13 percent of Americans believed that air conditioning in a car was a necessity; today, most cannot imagine life without it. (14) One of the traps of "progress" is that once you move forward it is extremely difficult to go back. However, a growing number of people, from all incomes and backgrounds, are tired of the consumption lifestyle and want to drop out of the cycle of spending to belong. The challenge these individuals face is whether or not they will be able to summon the courage to ignore a possible negative reaction from their peer groups and consumptive communities.

The first step that you can take is to start talking to people about financial matters. Talk to colleagues at work, friends in your neighbourhood, and other parents and families. You will be shocked at how many people share your concerns. I know this is a difficult subject to address given that many people are uncomfortable talking about finances—many people would rather discuss their love lives, religion, or politics than money. Summoning the courage to bring up a controversial topic is always difficult, especially when it comes to money, yet I assure you that for every objection you receive, you will have two or three supporters. A second step is to create a monthly financial conversation circle. You can discuss topics ranging from how to reduce household expenses, to healthy and economical eating, to creative gift ideas, to exciting economical holidays, to specific financial topics such as retirement, estate, and insurance planning. What you are basically creating is a new consumptive community, only this one wants and has a vested interest in improving your financial well-being.

One of the simplest ways to avoid the "new necessities" and save more is to decrease the amount of television you watch. Harvard Professor Juliet Schor found that the more TV a person watches, the more he or she tends to spend. Other research has also found a correlation between indebtedness and excessive TV viewing. (6) A possible explanation for these findings is that television, through its ability to skillfully combine language, imagery, and social references, and bypass income and cultural barriers, inflates our sense of what is a normal and expected standard of living. (3) The goal of television programming is to ensure that viewers become discontent with some aspect of their lives. This discontentment could manifest itself in revealing a desire to renovate, landscape, travel, or purchase a new vehicle. In reducing your viewing time, you are essentially becoming more content with what you have, as you are no longer exposed to the constant reminders of your numerous inadequacies. The financial benefits of this cutback in viewing time are numerous. You'll notice these benefits as your self-confidence improves and your spending to belong subsides.

I would also encourage you to keep track of your spending on the "new necessities" to get an idea of the financial costs you are incurring. One of the best exercises to discover where your money is disappearing and to gain a clearer picture of your spending habits is to keep a little notepad with you. Keep this notepad with you at all times, and write down the item and amount that you spend anytime you purchase anything (both big and small). Although this may seem tedious, in sticking with this exercise for roughly two months, you will discover vast amounts of wasteful and non-priority spending. Your data will quickly reveal to you the areas of your regular spending and into what category your purchases ought to go. After an honest analysis, you will be able to better prioritize your spending. In essence, you are awakening your financial conscious.

The pressure of spending to belong has become an unfortunate part of everyday life. The "new necessities," pressure from advertisers, consumptive communities, positional goods, and new consumer research all add up to an economy that Tamara Draut, author of *Strapped: Why America's 20- and 30-Somethings Can't Get Ahead*, says is increasingly stacked against us. The combination of this pressure to consume, in conjunction with an increasing array of new products to consume, has been financially lethal. The evolution and consumption pressure of the consumer society has resulted in smart, hard-working, well-intended individuals and their families spending beyond their means in the quest to belong. Exposing the Money Assassins, their tactics, and intentions is a key step in the process of rebuilding our financial mindset. My hope is that this chapter has brought about an awareness of current practices and pressures within the consumer society, giving individuals a chance to build financial immunity against them.

Part One of the book was designed to be prescriptive in nature and create a sense of awareness of some of the overarching, macro issues that have been influencing the financial thoughts and behaviour of individuals. Before we could delve into typical financial "know-how," we had to understand why so many of us were struggling in an era with so much wealth. We started with learning valuable lessons from the financial survivors of our past and discovered the relevance of tried and true financial advice such as the value of financial empathy, thrift, and frugality. We questioned the true meaning of wealth and dispelled the myth that more money means more happiness. We showed how technology has not served us well in our attempt to become financially mature, and we saw the value of using cash and avoiding plastic. We saw how children are being used to influence and increase family spending. We saw how marketers and advertisers exploit our weaknesses and how the "new necessities" have increased the baseline cost of living. In essence, we have seen how our economic system has evolved to work against us, how debt has enslaved us, and how technology has allowed us to spend more of our money faster.

Part One of the book offers important suggestions and strategies to recapture financial freedom from a belief and philosophical perspective. It is in Part Two, where we turn our attention to now, that we will tackle the big issues that are needed to reclaim our financial freedom. We will discover free money, we will reclaim financial common sense related to home buying, we will eliminate debt, and we will rediscover pearls of financial wisdom. These practical financial lessons and solutions to our problems are certain to reduce the burden of debt and create a life full of wealth.

Chapter 5
Living "Car-Lite":
The Discovery of Free Money

You should read this chapter if:
> *Your goal is to retire in your forties*
> *You're fed up with high gas prices*
> *You worry about money*
> *You have credit card debt, student loans, or personal loans*
> *You long for the freedom and serenity of a debt-free lifestyle*
> *You rent and want to save for a down payment for a house*
> *You want to pay off your mortgage early*
> *You just want to work less and have more fun!*
— Chris Balish, author of *How to Live Well Without Owning a Car*

Second only to our homes, vehicles serve as the greatest threat to our financial freedom and well-being. Since the 1950s, most North American cities have been developed to foster a car-dependant culture. Currently, the majority of North American families own two or more vehicles. Few people are aware of the cumulative costs of owning and operating these vehicles and the potential for adverse effects that vehicle ownership can have on their financial well-being. Fortunately, this harm can be minimized by adopting one or more simple strategies to live "car-lite." (1)

The purchase and maintenance costs of a single vehicle, including insurance, gas, and general upkeep, consume approximately 15–20 percent of the average earner's gross income. Put another way, 20 percent of our work time is devoted to financing an object that sits idle for the vast majority of the day. Vehicles are a major contributor to spending beyond our means, leading to higher levels of debt and fewer savings. This is a high price to pay for convenience. Vehicles regularly comprise one of our first major expenditures, which is why an earlier awareness of their potential financial consequences can assist in our long-term financial health. Let us examine this in greater detail.

The first step is to calculate the impact of vehicle ownership and operation on your monthly budget. These costs are highly variable between individuals and families, and in the following example, we will use conservative estimates of monthly payments. I would encourage you to calculate your own monthly personal costs. The results may surprise you!

Monthly Operational Costs

$400 Vehicle Payment	**_____Your Payment**
$125 Vehicle Insurance	**_____Your Insurance**
$150 Gas	**_____Your Gas Bill**
$125 Maintenance	**_____Your Maintenance Expense**

In adding together the monthly operational costs of a vehicle, we get a monthly total of $800. It is important to note that these figures do not include depreciation costs and parking expenses, which likely amount to $200 and $50–$200 (city dependant) per month, respectively. With total monthly costs above $1,000, the average vehicle owner is likely to spend over $12,000 per year for the privilege of driving. This number can be doubled for the average two-car family. Using an annual cost of $12,000, the simple table below illustrates the percentage of income allocated towards owning and operating a single vehicle, relative to a variety of income levels. After taking into account the effects of income taxation, this percentage is even higher. Determining your vehicle expenditures to income ratio is a key component to understanding and improving your financial plan. Do it now!

Gross Income	Percentage of Income Allocated to Vehicle
$35,000	29%
$45,000	23%
$55,000	19%
$65,000	15%

If your ratio is 20 percent or greater, ask yourself if it is worth working one day of every week, or one out of every five years of your life just for the privilege of owning a vehicle. In addition, achieving a savings target of 20–30% of gross income becomes more difficult when a sizeable percentage of your income is devoted to vehicle-related spending. If your ratio is less than or near 10 percent, congratulations, as you have discovered an important secret to financial success and freedom. However, for those whose ratio nears 20 percent or greater, there is no need to despair, as you have just discovered one of the greatest and simplest opportunities to turn your finances around!

What is simple is not always easy. To reclaim your financial well-being and reduce your debt, you must first be prepared to envision a different lifestyle. Re-examining large expenditures such as a vehicle is a great place to start; however, it is worth first examining how and why our society systematically underestimates the expense of vehicles and their subsequent financial consequences. In his book, *How to Live Well Without Owning a Car*, Chris Balish writes, "This lack of understanding is fueled by an endless barrage of automobile advertising purposely designed to make cars seem more affordable than they really are." Marketers have done an exceptional job of convincing the public of the merits of owning a product that sits idle for 90 percent of the day, pollutes the environment, causes stress and road rage, has the potential to compromise physical health, and all the while consumes 20 percent of our hard-earned money.

The automobile industry is the largest buyer of advertising in the world, accounting for nearly 20 percent of all advertising spending. (1) This level of spending is fuelled by the highly competitive nature of the auto industry and, more important, the need to immerse the public in a culture where cars are deemed a necessity. With billions of dollars of profit at stake, the industry goes to great lengths to convince the public that cars or SUVs are an essential part of life. Advertisers exploit our desires for image, status, sex, power, and prestige, all key ingredients to successful vehicle marketing campaigns. While safety and functionality are commonly cited as the main motivators of vehicle purchases, industry research and focus groups reveal image as an overriding determinant. With this in mind, it is easy to understand how strong emotional feelings overpower financial common sense.

Car manufacturers prey on the vulnerabilities and feelings of inadequacy of individuals and families, with U.S. automobile prices up 75 percent since the 1990s. (3) The public willingness to pay stems partly from the advertisers' success in promoting vehicles as part of the family. In her book *Can't Buy My Love*, Jean Kilbourne writes about how one Honda advertisement shows a wallet with two pictures, one displaying the children and family dog, the other showing off the family vehicle. The caption on the ad reads, "If anybody should ask, go ahead and show them your pride and joy. The Civic 4-Door." (2) Kilbourne sites another similar advertisement for Jaguar: "It has its mother's eyes, its father's stature and its brother's appetite for mischief." (2) When in doubt, advertisers know that people will also pay a premium for sex. In one study, men rated the car as more appealing, more expensive-looking, faster, and better when the car was promoted by a seductive model, as opposed to men who saw the same ad without the model. (4)

Society's relationship with the automobile industry goes beyond the influence of the advertising industry. Our indoctrination into car culture starts at a young age. Most children are raised in two-car families, play with Hot Wheels, and dream of one day being able to drive. Long before reaching the legal driving age, many children are able to recognize familiar automobile brands, advertisements, and symbols. Many young people seek part-time employment in order to purchase a vehicle. And when they do get their car, they often opt for a flashier, more expensive car with an accompanying sound system instead of buying a more compact, fuel efficient, or even second-hand car.

To break free from the ties of financial enslavement, many of us will need to undergo a change in our lifestyle where vehicles will play a significantly smaller role. While this change may be difficult, it is possible. In fact, the immediate and long-term financial rewards and significant personal health benefits far outweigh the challenges posed. While some are able to live well without owning or operating a vehicle, this may not be feasible or practical for most. I am not insisting that everyone cease using their vehicles, but I am advocating that we relegate our cars to a secondary place in our lives where they serve us, rather than continue on in a situation where we work and spend to serve them.

To make this change, we need to strive to achieve the lifestyle that Balish terms "car-lite." In financial terms, this can be translated into reducing your transportation expenditures from 20 to 10 percent of your gross income. For both individuals and families, this means reducing your dependence on your automobile as the primary, and in many cases only, form of transportation. This can be accomplished in a number of ways, including transitioning from a two-car to a one-car family, reducing annual driving by half, downsizing to a vehicle valued at 20 percent rather than 40 percent of your annual income, and choosing alternate forms of transportation such as car sharing or pooling, biking, walking, or taking public transportation. Before examining these options in greater detail, let us explore the financial incentives by expanding on the example used above.

Imagine an individual with no dependants who is 23 years of age, is starting his or her first job, and will earn $40,000 per year. Eight thousand dollars (20% of their income), or $667 per month, will be spent on financing vehicle expenditures. Living "car-lite" would mean reducing these figures to 10%, or $4,000 per year, equaling $333 per month. If the amount saved was then invested, even in a very conservative high-interest savings account at 3.5 percent, this would translate into savings of $35,000 eight years later, the average length of owning a vehicle. (5) Alternatively, if this money went into retirement savings, it would be worth almost $450,000 at age 60! In the shorter term, this money could be used to meet commonly cited but previously eluded goals, including debt reduction, shorter work hours, more vacations, or saving for a home down payment without resorting to a 30- to 40-year mortgage.

Now imagine a double income family that earns $100,000 per year, with spousal salaries of $60,000 and $40,000, respectively. To accommodate the family transportation needs, they own and operate two vehicles, spending on average $20,000 per year on their combined vehicles. Transitioning to a "car-lite" lifestyle would free up $10,000 per year, or $838 per month. Invested in the same 3.5 percent savings account, this would earn the family almost $90,000 over an eight-year period. The opportunities for this money are endless, including a family sabbatical, retirement or children's education funds, vacation property, charitable donations, or the opportunity to transition into a new career or return to school. The options are empowering!

If the money saved and options gained sound enticing, then it may well be worthwhile to invest in the effort required to commit to a "car-lite" lifestyle. Several key factors will assist in this successful transition, namely understanding and applying the concept of "location efficiency," embracing alternative forms of transportation, and re-evaluating the role that automobiles play in our lives. The concept of "location efficiency" is based on the idea of maximizing the use of your community surroundings, including where you live, work, and shop, with the main goal of accommodating one car per family. Location efficiency can be optimized by living within walking or cycling distance of the workplace, children's schools, or the grocery store, or in proximity to major public transportation routes, all with the aim of minimizing automobile dependency. While it is often not possible to incorporate all of these simultaneously, the idea is to make a concerted effort to live in an environment where use of the existing infrastructure is maximized.

In his book, Balish asks the question: Wouldn't it be great if someone invented a form of personal transportation that was basically free; available when you wanted and needed it; required no taxes, parking, or registration fees; and was not susceptible to high gas prices? Of course the answer is yes, and this invention is available at your nearest bicycle shop! Cycling is commonly used all around the world as a viable and efficient form of transportation, and most major cities house a cycling advocacy group that promotes bike commuting and safety.

In many settings, cycling and public transportation are seen as vehicles for children and the poor, where automobiles are viewed as the vehicle that embodies freedom, control, and power. *Men's Health* magazine describes it differently, stating, "Your car is no longer a chariot of freedom; it's a money-sucking horse that gets you to the office." (1) In addition to its financial toll, we now spend more time commuting than on our physical fitness or hobbies. We also consistently rank commuting as the largest waste of time, and although we claim that climate change is our deepest public concern, we continue to pollute through the oil processing and CO_2 emissions required for fuelling our vehicles. (1) Paul Hawken, author of *The Ecology of Commerce*, points out that after dividing all the car mileage driven in a year by the time spent supporting and maintaining vehicles, we end up travelling no faster than the speed of a bicycle. (6) In addition to the financial benefits of cycling, the physical health benefits are extensive. The average bicycle commuter loses 13 pounds within the first year of implementing this lifestyle change. While commuter cycling may not be feasible for everyone and might lack some prestige, it is a viable option that betters our physical health, helps the environment, improves our finances, and ultimately enables us to spend less time in the workplace, thus providing us greater flexibility to pursue family and leisure activities.

It is likely that many readers will already be compiling a mental list of the challenges and drawbacks to alternative modes of transportation. This will include flashbacks of the time they just missed the bus and had to wait another 15 minutes in the rain or blowing snow, or when they were nearly hit by that crazy driver while biking to work. However, as Harvard psychologist Daniel Gilbert explains, these "least likely" or rare experiences are often the ones we most readily recall, leading us to mistakenly conclude that these experiences are more common than they actually are. We then "mistakenly expect the experience [i.e. taking the bus] to be much more inconvenient and frustrating than it likely" is. (7) The transition to incorporating and eventually maximizing alternative forms of transportation requires time, patience, trial and error, and a firm commitment to change. Before rushing out to sell your vehicle, take the time to try out these various alternatives to help foster a successful transition to "car-lite."

In some circles our peers, associates, and friends may view our choice to downsize our vehicle or use public transportation as a sign of tough financial times. Unfortunately, some may mistakenly see this change as a step backwards. The often unanticipated bruising of our ego or pride demonstrates the degree to which self-image is invested in or attached to our vehicles. Those transitioning to a "car-lite" lifestyle may fear criticism or mockery from shortsighted peers or colleagues who have difficulty understanding why one would voluntarily make these changes. Responding with "I now have the option to work four days a week," "I am saving ten to twenty percent more for early retirement," or "I can now afford an annual dream vacation!" will go a long way to silencing the critics, and may even serve as a catalyst to enable a similar change among a previously reluctant or fearful colleague.

> *Smart cars may be smart, but walking, cycling, and using transit will always be smarter!*
> —*Chad Viminitz*

Contemplating a reduced reliance on vehicle ownership may incite concerns about times when immediate transportation or temporary multi-day stretches are required. In these cases, consideration should be given to using cabs, vehicle sharing, and rental agencies. When used infrequently, vehicle sharing and rentals serve as an extremely convenient, efficient, and cost-effective way to accommodate temporary stretches where a vehicle is required.

Where vehicle use is needed, the question often arises as to whether it is economically preferable to purchase or lease. While the tax advantages for business owners and the self-employed may favour leasing, purchasing and keeping the same vehicle for ten or more years is the optimal strategy for most readers. For the majority, leasing serves to up-scale a vehicle beyond what one could otherwise afford, with over half of its advertised benefits centred on image and convenience. Many choose larger, less fuel-efficient, or premium fuel vehicles, placing a greater financial burden on themselves in an era of rapidly rising fuel costs. Leasing promotes the concepts of financial invincibility and the perception of wealth. While initial monthly payments and upfront costs may be lower, these fixed payments continue beyond the usual three- to five-year period where those in a buying agreement typically end. Rather than owning the vehicle, the leaser continues the endless cycle of debt-generating monthly payments. While there is typically the option to purchase the vehicle at the end of the lease term, the cited value is commonly much higher than its actual worth. Most have not saved for this purchase and are forced to re-enter the lease cycle. While some argue that the difference between the lease and buying costs can be saved and invested, this rarely comes to fruition, as most find other ways to spend the difference.

At the end of the day, the type of vehicle you own is of little importance if two general rules are followed. First, the importance of achieving a one-vehicle family cannot be overstated. Second, individuals and/or families should strive to reduce their total annual vehicle expense to 10 percent, and certainly below 15 percent, of their gross annual income. The ultimate financial goal of a "car-lite" lifestyle is to free up 5–10 percent of gross income in order to get one step closer to achieving a savings target of 20–30 percent! After completing the transition to living "car-lite," you will realize that society's dependency on automobiles "is a psychological addiction, not a physical one." (1) Our lives, family, time, and energy are far too precious to be spent supporting an addiction to the almighty automobile. Break free and reap the personal and financial rewards of living "car-lite."

Chapter 6

Home Cent$

The decision to buy a home is the single greatest determinant of the long-term financial fate of individuals and families. Given the size of the original financial outlay, and the commitment to recurring expenses including utilities, upkeep, property taxes, insurance, landscaping, furnishing, and decorating, this is easy to understand. As such, home ownership warrants special attention, as caution is needed to avoid both planned and unplanned home expenditures that can quickly redirect monthly cash flow away from your financial plan. With so much excitement and anticipation surrounding home ownership, it is unfortunate that this process serves as the beginning of a life of financial entrapment for many. Thankfully, this can be avoided by considering and applying a few sound financial principles.

Advice about home buying is often difficult to convey given a lack of black and white rules. However, this chapter will address some basic guidelines, with a focus on first-time homebuyers, home upgraders, and those seeking to free up cash and reduce debt. We will also explore strategies to avoid becoming "house rich" and "cash poor," to save effectively for a down payment, and to determine the mortgage payment that a financial plan can withstand.

The long-term financial implications of home ownership are commonly ignored because of emotional factors, misinformation, and a lack of planning. Emotions are the key driver, as a home is naturally seen, first and foremost, as a comfortable place to live, raise a family, create memories, and establish roots. It is clear that lifestyle factors, including location, perceived community safety, yard size, square footage, and the number of bedrooms and bathrooms factor heavily into the decision. While financial factors such as price, interest rates, down payment, and mortgage terms do come into play in the end, it is often the emotional response to the lifestyle factors that ultimately drive home purchases.

The financial realities of buying and owning a home can be overwhelming. Given the extent of monetary resources at stake, it is hard to believe that nearly 80 percent of first-time homebuyers never seek financial advice. (1) When advice is sought, it often comes in the middle of the purchasing process, when emotions are running high. This lack of planning can promote misinformation and a tendency to financially overcommit.

Let us now examine some general guidelines.

Know Your Limit

To ensure optimal financial freedom, flexibility, and control, maintaining one's total debt service ratio (TDSR) below 30 percent is essential. TDSR is a vital concept that warrants a brief explanation, as it will be referred to in the following chapters. The TDSR is often used by lending institutions, such as banks, to determine whether or not they will lend you money. Your TDSR is calculated by taking your monthly mortgage payment plus any vehicle payment; other debt payments including credit cards, lines of credit, student loans, etc.; heating; taxes; and condo fees. Add up all those monthly payments and divide them by your gross (before tax) monthly income.

Calculating Your Total Debt Service Ratio

Please note that this form can also be found on the Money Assassins website, *www.moneyassassins.com*.

Monthly Mortgage Payment $_____

Monthly Vehicle Payment $_____

Monthly Debt Payments (student loan,
    credit card, line of credit) $_____

Monthly Heating, Taxes, Condo fees $_____

Divided by Monthly Gross Income
    (before tax) $_____

It is crucial to realize that the amount a lending institution will lend you has absolutely nothing to do with what is right for your financial plan. This ratio only reflects the level of risk that the lending institution is prepared to accord you and should never be interpreted as the suggested amount that you should accept in your plan. The level of comfort amongst lending institutions has changed significantly over time. During most of the twentieth century, bankers were only comfortable lending up to a TDSR of 20 percent, where this figure was only based on the income of the male in the household. Today, however, lenders are comfortable lending up to a 40 percent ratio based on the combined household incomes of a couple. Home ownership, including mortgage payments, property taxes, utilities, and condominium fees, typically comprises two-thirds of your overall TDSR, and is the largest obstacle to maintaining this ratio within the 20 percent range.

Individuals are confronted with a moment of truth when the bank or lending institution discloses the size of the approved mortgage. Serving as a critical financial crossroads, the ensuing financial decision can ultimately define your financial life. Depending on other existing debt, banks and lending institutions will commonly provide a loan that allows for house-related expenditures, the largest portion being your mortgage payment, of nearly 32 percent of your income. When other debts such as vehicle payments, student lines, or credit lines are included, your total debt servicing ratio is allowed to reach 40 percent. However, approval for a mortgage that puts an individual near a 40 percent TDSR is only an indication of the maximum level of risk that the bank or lending institution is willing to incur, not a financial recommendation.

Unfortunately, most have not sought previous financial advice or planning and the interaction with the lending agent constitutes their lone source of advice. The advice is misconstrued as an endorsement from a financial planning perspective and mistakenly assumed that the upper limit of borrowing is synonymous with what you can comfortably afford. The majority overcommit to a super-sized mortgage, while very few take the road less travelled by accepting a modest mortgage and following a road paved with financial prudence. Financial institutions profit heavily from the practice of lending as much money as possible, and employees are advised to maximize loans within the organization's comfort of risk. It is tragic that the financial lives of many are determined by a lending officer, whose vested interests lies with serving the company rather than with customizing lending to customers' comprehensive financial plans.

It is safe to say that the lower the TDSR the better. While there is no absolute value for the optimal TDSR, a range of 20–29 percent serves as a compromise between what is realistic for most and what will still allow for a reasonable amount of financial flexibility and security. To accomplish this, house-related costs should not exceed a TDSR of 22 percent. This translates into a mortgage that is *no greater* than 2.5 times, and ideally between 1.5 and 2.0 times, the household income. The following table highlights the maximum recommended mortgage value for a range of household incomes.

Total Household Income	Recommended Mortgage Amount
$50,000	$125,000
$100,000	$250,000
$130,000	$325,000

Maintaining a TDSR target within the range of 20–29 percent could well mean delaying the purchase of that dream home, having to rent a little longer to save for a down payment, or even having to downsize from your current home. However, the upside cannot be overstated. Rarely calculated in the cost of owing a home, beyond regular mortgage payments, are the ongoing costs of owning larger and more expensive homes. One can expect higher utility bills and higher property taxes, but the largest cost that most do not consider is the price associated with a new, possibly more expensive, consumer cohort. As we discussed earlier, people who live, work, and socialize in similar environments will spend money similarly and will intuitively demand certain consumption standards of each other in order to belong to the group. Social pressure to ensure that your yard is kept up to neighbourhood standards, that you drive an acceptable vehicle, that you have satisfactory home décor, and that you participate in social functions and community events are just a few examples. These expected and ongoing costs will redirect thousands of dollars away from your financial plan, but will be easily justified as simply normal expenses of life.

The dangers of having an overextended TDSR are numerous. A major concern with having your TDSR near the upper limit is that you are now exposed to interest rate risks. A typical mortgage term spans a five-year period into which most are locked. Interest rates will inevitably change throughout this period, the implications of which are often not discussed during the application process. When the mortgage is up for renewal at term's end, rates may well have increased. Depending on the size of the mortgage, a seemingly minimal increase in rates can result in a major increase in payments. For example, a 3 percent rise in interest rates can result in a mortgage payment increase that ranges from $200 to $1,000 per month. To make up the difference, options include allocating more income to the payments and cutting other spending, or incurring more debt. Over the life span of the mortgage, this can amount to tens of thousands of extra dollars. If you are overextended with a TDSR at or near the upper limit, there is no room to maneuver and no cushion to absorb these changes. Avoid this financial anxiety, a leading cause of chronic stress, by allowing yourself room to incur extra costs by maintaining a TDSR below 30 percent.

Maintaining a TDSR in the 20 percent range greatly reduces the anxieties of unexpected or unplanned financial strains. A common scenario arises when a young, dual-income couple maximizes the mortgage on their first home, reaching a TDSR at or near 40 percent. Home ownership expenses are manageable until a few years later when the couple decides to start a family. What happens if they prefer that one parent stays at home with the children? A dual-income-based mortgage payment is now reduced to one. In the absence of a cushion, this may be unfeasible or will occur at the cost of great stress and anxiety. A similar situation arises in the case of a change in employment with less expected income, a desire to pursue further education, ever-increasing heating bills, and an unexpected illness—one of the top reasons for foreclosure on homes today. The stress of a large mortgage commitment can be smothering.

The results of minimizing one's total debt service ratio can be life-altering. While this is not always easy, it is entirely feasible, largely by resisting the temptation of a mortgage beyond 2.5 times the household income and rejecting the initial pre-approved mortgage offer from your lender. For those who have not yet committed to home ownership, it is far easier to know your mortgage limit before visiting the lender and committing to the TDSR in the 20 percent range. For those who already find themselves "house rich" and "cash poor," it is never too late to make a significant financial change by downsizing. While this may not be easy, the long-term payoffs will be worth the initial struggles.

Many readers may be wondering, "But I thought investing in a home was your best investment?" I am not disputing the value and potential financial benefits of home ownership, but with 30- to 40-year mortgages, home lines of credit, increased heating costs, furnishing larger homes, and more decorative landscaping, buying a home cannot be taken for granted as the guaranteed sound investment it once was.

Canadians Beware of the Home Buyers' Plan

In February, 1992, the Canadian government established the Home Buyers' Plan (HBP), a program that was intended to last a year. Its inception came at the tail end of the 1990–1991 recession and was designed as a strategy to boost the economy through the promotion of home starts and sales. Most individuals and families lacked the needed disposable income for a down payment on a home but did have thousands of dollars invested in their Registered Retirement Savings Plans (RRSPs). The plan allowed for potential homebuyers to withdraw RRSP savings towards a home down payment. The plan was a success, boosting housing starts and, ultimately, the economy. The HBP was thus made into a permanent plan. Today, the HBP is restricted to first-time homebuyers and currently has a maximum RRSP withdrawal limit of $25,000. Unfortunately, what was intended as a short-term strategy to boost a recessed economy is all too commonly misused as a financial strategy for funding down payments. Let us examine its pitfalls.

Many Canadians have followed sound financial advice to start RRSPs early, committing to a long-term savings plan with the best of intentions. But then changes occur. People get married, begin careers, and have children. Suddenly, buying a home becomes a top priority. With a new sense of urgency, first-time homebuyers begin to frantically search for ways to afford a down payment. With little or no available savings, and only long-term RRSPs in hand, realtors, mortgage lenders, and financial advisors commonly suggest that clients use the HBP. Although their intentions are good, many advisors will encourage their clients to use the plan to buy a home, giving advice that is not always the most financially prudent course of action. The enthusiasm of home ownership quickly displaces the once-noble goal of long-term retirement savings.

The benefits of the HBP are highly touted. The option for a tax-free withdrawal from an RRSP, serving as an interest-free loan from you to yourself with little paperwork and a lengthy fifteen-year repayment period, are all notable advantages. It is therefore understandable why thousands of Canadians have opted to use the plan, especially given the endorsement from so many professionals. Unfortunately, as the saying goes, "if it sounds too good to be true, it probably is." With the excitement and anticipation of buying a first home, few are advised of the dangers and drawbacks of the plan. Disadvantages can include possible losses of investments, unanticipated sales charges, delayed retirement, and probable tax consequences, to name but a few. Home ownership is a worthy goal, but funding the down payment from RRSP savings is often long-term pain for short-term gain. Let's examine some of the potential drawbacks in more detail.

Appropriately, many individuals invest in RRSPs in their 20s and 30s, taking advantage of a long investment time horizon, a key and crucial element to successful investing. This long investment time horizon maximizes the power of compound interest and allows for more aggressive portfolios to weather inevitable market fluctuations. However, when you suddenly want to make an unexpected withdrawal from your RRSPs, you make yourself and your money vulnerable to the current state of the market and are often then forced to sell at a loss. In addition, young investors may incur extra fees if the investment funds were set up with deferred sales charges. These are commonly in effect for the first six years of a plan. The penalty for early withdrawal can typically range from 1 to 6 percent of the portfolio's value, depending on what year the withdrawal was made.

Probably the biggest downside to using the HBP is the loss of compound interest, which is rarely calculated or discussed, and can add up to a very substantial amount. Withdrawing $20,000 from your RRSP and being out of the investment market for fifteen years or longer has cumulative and long-lasting effects that cannot be reversed. Take for example a young couple in their early 30s who wish to retire at age 60. The removal of $20,000 from each RRSP account, even if paid back over fifteen years, amounts to over $250,000 in lost retirement savings at age 60. In addition to the hundreds of thousands of lost retirement savings, there is also the risk of higher taxes and lost RRSP contribution room. The HBP requires the borrower to begin repayment within two years after the initial withdrawal. If the full $25,000 is withdrawn, a minimum annual payment of $1,666.66 is required. One report showed that one-third of HBP participants do not make this required payment. As family-related costs expand, and the pressure to "keep up with the Joneses" intensifies, additional payments become all the more difficult. If the required minimum payment is neglected, the $1,666.66 is added to that year's income and is fully taxed. The tax paid will most likely be greater than the original tax deduction, as your tax bracket is usually greater in future years than at the time of the original RRSP contribution. Of even greater alarm is that if the minimum amount is not repaid, the RRSP contribution room is lost forever. Given the important role RRSPs play as one of the greatest and most lucrative ways for Canadians to save for retirement, any lost opportunity to use this tax-deferring tool is of major concern. Retirement wealth relies on both steady RRSP contributions and steady growth within those investments. If that base amount is reduced through withdrawals, growth is jeopardized, and imposed annual RRSP contribution limits prohibit recovery for these losses. These adverse effects on retirement savings are rarely considered when overshadowed by the excitement of being a new homeowner. If home ownership is anticipated, it is well worth taking the time and discipline to invest in a separate short-term savings plan to fund a down payment. The Canadian government's new Tax Free Savings Account would be a great place to begin, which is explored in greater detail in Chapter Eight. The benefits are more control and reduced stress resulting from a strengthened financial position. It cannot be overemphasized that the Home Buyers' Plan is not a savings strategy to fund a down payment, as this was never its intention. Rather, it serves to enable last-minute financing for the financially ill-prepared. Plan ahead and avoid potential investment losses, extra taxes, service charges, and long-term consequences of lost contribution room and, ultimately, a delayed retirement.

Housing Behaviour

When I ask people about the best financial decision they have ever made, the most common response is "my education" or "my home." Unfortunately, for most people in the early stages of their professional careers, these are often the only large-scale financial investments they have made. In many cases, these will also be the only investments that many people will ever make. Education and home ownership are also the only investments that society deems to be worthy of indebtedness. This acceptance of indebtedness in the pursuit of higher education or to buy a home helps explain why so many will borrow to pay for these purchases. From a traditional perspective, both are worthy of debt, as they required personal sacrifice and long-term planning to achieve. In today's context, however, the personal sacrifices and need to develop long-term plans in order to pursue higher education or purchase a home are not what they once were.

Principle residences tend to be a good investment for three reasons. The first reason is the power of leveraging or borrowing to invest. An individual can buy an asset worth $300,000 for as little as 0–10 percent down. For example, a 5 percent increase on the value of a $300,000 home equates to $15,000, making the home appear to be a good investment. On the other hand, if retirement investments return a generous and not routine 15%, three times that of your home, the gain on a $1,000 account is a paltry $150. This figure is surely nothing to get excited about compared to the $15,000 return on the home. When we see these large dollar amounts, we begin to compare absolute returns to relative returns. Even though the retirement investment offered three times the return compared to the home, many feel that the real estate was the better investment—it's not! If you look at long-term real estate rates of return, you will notice there are other asset classes that have been far more successful. According to the 2006 Canadian Andex Chart, a chart that shows graphical representation of a broad spectrum of economic data, shows that from 1980 to 2006, the average return on real estate in Canada was 5.9 percent, with Vancouver, Toronto, and Calgary registering returns of 7.5 percent, 6.3 percent, and 5.5 percent, respectively. Since 1970, the Canadian stock market has generated returns of over 10 percent.

The second reason why principle residences are good investments is because of the preferential tax treatment they receive. In Canada, we do not pay any tax on the annual growth of the value of our home, nor do we pay any tax if we decide to sell it. This is different from other investments in that we usually have to pay taxes on an annual basis and upon the sale of these assets. It is important to note that this preferential tax treatment does not apply to any recreational or rental property, only to your principle residence. The tax that is due on other properties comes in the form of capital gains and is due in the tax year in which you sell. So as an investment, your principle residence, which is exempt from taxes, has a significant advantage over other taxable investments that attract interest, dividend, or capital gains income. Again, it is not necessarily the real estate itself that explains the investment returns, but rather the tax treatment accorded to the asset. When looking at other investments, the above example reveals the importance of examining the associated tax considerations, as they can make the difference between a good investment and a mediocre one.

The third reason that explains the value of investing in a principle residence is best explained by investment guru Warren Buffet: "Diversification may preserve wealth, but concentration builds wealth." Therefore, investing $300,000 into a single asset, in this case a home, means that the returns will be high if this asset appreciates significantly. Yet caution should be exercised, as the downside is also true. If you invest all of your money into your home and the market declines, you will lose a significant amount of money. Since a home is usually the largest asset we own, we tend to make a substantial personal commitment to ensure that our decision to purchase our home is well-researched. Yet we are also willing to invest our personal time into the upkeep and improvement of the home, as we usually take personal pride in our ownership. This pride and investment of time is rarely evident in the maintenance of our investment portfolio or financial plans but could provide for significant rewards as well.

When prices are on the rise in the housing market, we often feel pressured to get into the market if we are not already in it. A hot housing market will bring up comments such as: "I have been renting for the past couple of years. The real estate market is really hot right now and I am scared that if I don't get in now, I won't be able to afford to buy a home in the future." Although this fear may be understandable, buying high and being motivated by fear almost never indicate a good time to invest. The fear of never being able to own your own home, and the stigma that goes with it, are strong emotional motivators for many. However, according to Buffet, "Be fearful when others are greedy and greedy when others are fearful." Many young people find themselves swept into the housing market before they are truly ready. Make sure that you take the time before you decide to buy a home. Reflect on your reasons for buying and ensure they are the right reasons for you and your family.

Ironically, when the stock market undergoes a strong run of five or more years, we do not feel the same urgency to get into the investment market. Nor do we hear about people frantically looking to get into the investment market before it's too late. This is largely because housing prices are not reported daily in the news and do not flash across the business pages. Because we all need a place to live, reports of sinking housing prices do not drive us into the same panic mode as when prices drop in the investment markets. Ignoring short-term news and reports related to investment portfolios is good advice to follow.

For many, a home is first and foremost a place to live, gather with friends, and potentially raise a family. We don't typically manage or handle our home like other investments such as stocks or mutual funds. For example, if you had an investment that tripled over a two-year period, you would most likely sell it. If a specific investment you liked suddenly became a good buying opportunity, you would invest more. But in the context of your home, these options are simply not available. There is no doubt that a home has the potential to be a great investment, but that does not mean it's financially prudent to overextend your mortgage commitment at the expense of your overall financial plan.

Housing Expectations

For many Canadians, the dream of owning a home begins at an early age. Many of us have imagined living in a condo overlooking the mountains or water, or in a 2,000-square-foot home with an extra room and fireplace, or in a cool apartment in the heart of a bustling city. Although we may still aspire to fulfill our earlier goals of purchasing that special home, we must remember that these are but descriptions of a physical place to live. I am sure that most of my readers would agree that a home is much more than the unique architecture, funky gadgets, or fancy décor. A home is created with love, passion, peace of mind, friendship, and hospitality. For millions of people around the world, fabulous homes have been created in condos, multiple-family dwellings, and apartments. Of course a house can be a wonderful home, but it is worth both our time and money to explore other financial and sustainable options.

To develop a stronger financial plan, it is imperative that we change our perspectives regarding home ownership. A key element in changing this perspective is first and foremost in recognizing that financial indebtedness is not the only way to create a home. Part of the problem is that our expectation of what a home should be have outstripped the ability for many of us to afford one. These unrealistic expectations are the root of much of today's financial stress and anxiety. Many of our expectations are no longer in alignment with any clear sense of financial reality. In the 1950s, the average-sized home was 1,000 square feet and mortgages never exceeded three times the salary of the homeowner. (2) Today, many people are starting their careers in their late 20s or early 30s. This is a significant change from only a generation ago. However, while these "latecomers" may not have rushed to get into the workforce, many of them have high expectations when it comes to purchasing their first home. It is now commonplace for first-time buyers to expect to have a 2,000-square-foot starter home filled with stainless steel appliances, a den, a great room, an attached garage, and a master bedroom with a walk-in closet and an ensuite with a Jacuzzi tub.

As we discussed in Chapter Two, although these comforts of life may be nice, they have no connection with our goal of seeking happiness or well-being. Once the initial euphoria wears off and financial reality sets in, happiness becomes defined by an entirely different set of conditions. Memories and happiness in a home are built on solid relationships, love, laughter, health, friends, and family—all of which can be accomplished with less square footage, fewer appliances, and a smaller mortgage! Our constantly evolving high expectations lead us to incur enormous financial costs, not to mention a loss of control and flexibility in our lifestyles.

Let's look at two different families who have the same household income of $100,000 but very different expectations about what they want out of a home. Family A would like a larger, more expensive home, which translates into a greater monthly financial commitment, more spaces to fill in the home, and corresponding expectations of what high-priced gadgets are going to be put in the home. Buying into a more expensive neighbourhood may also change their consumptive community and peer group, perhaps leading to an increased level of spending in order to belong. Just like you should never buy the largest home on the block, you should also never have the highest TDSR on the block. If your mortgage is taking up your discretional income, you will not be able to visit, play, and vacation with your new friends and neighbours.

Family A: $300,000 mortgage; payment $1,920 (6 percent for 25 years); 2,000-square-foot home; 4 bedrooms; $0 additional savings by year 25; home valued at $1,287,500 (6 percent growth)

Family B: $200,000 mortgage; payment $1,280 (6 percent for 25 years); 1,200-square-foot home; 3 bedrooms; $520,000 in additional savings by year 25 (when investing the mortgage difference, not in RRSPs, and factoring in 8% compound interest); home valued at $858,300 (6 percent growth)

Family B not only has a home but also an additional half a million dollars in savings that provides them with more financial flexibility and control over their monthly cash flow, which will help them handle unexpected life circumstances or opportunities. Family A has a higher home value, but when $20,000 is needed, it is difficult to sell off only a portion of their home. This explains the recent popularity of home lines of credit that allow you to borrow against your equity. This, of course, is provided that you have equity, which is not always the case. I recommend that you always choose the financial option that gives you the most options and control over your financial future. In this case, purchasing a home with a smaller mortgage and saving the difference will almost certainly give you more options and greater control over your financial future.

Attaining a life of financial well-being requires that we change habits in our daily routines. As we discussed in "Living Car-Lite," location efficiency is an integral part of an integrated strategy to achieve financial well-being. Buying a home within your financial limits that is close to work, grocery stores, schools, and entertainment is an essential ingredient to enable you to have a degree of control over your financial future and be free of debt. It is interesting to note that in some major cities in the United States, "location efficient mortgages" are now available. These mortgages take into account the fact that the homeowner will spend less money on transportation and will therefore have more income to allocate towards a location-efficient home. Although the real estate mantra of "location, location, location" may be true, in terms of your principle residence, a better mantra might be "efficiency, efficiency, efficiency"; in our case, this stands for location efficiency, mortgage efficiency, resulting in financial efficiency.

Mortgage Amortization

Fewer and fewer people are able to contemplate an early retirement or slowing down and becoming less reliant on a monthly income. This is because more and more people are extending mortgage amortization periods beyond the traditional 25 years. One of the goals of financial planning is to provide people with greater flexibility for their monthly commitments. However, when people overcommit to a mortgage, they leave themselves with no options other than selling their home or incurring more debt. In the Canadian legal system, a life sentence for killing someone is 25 years, while signing up for a mortgage beyond 25 years can lead to a financial life sentence with no time off for good behaviour.

Below is a chart that reveals the total cost of interest alone on a $300,000 mortgage at 6 percent during amortization periods of 25, 35, and 40 years, respectively. I know 40-year mortgages are no longer available as I am writing this, but I would not be surprised to see them again in the future, so I have still included them.

25 years at 6%	35 years at 6%	40 years at 6%
$275,800	$412,000	$485,000

It is shocking to see that, by extending your amortization period beyond 25 years, the total interest cost will exceed the value of the original mortgage. In the case of this hypothetical mortgage, there is over a $200,000 difference between a 25-year and a 40-year mortgage. It is hard to believe that anyone would opt for the 40-year mortgage when you realize that the monthly difference in mortgage payments is just under $300. Always choose a mortgage amortization period of 25 years or less and avoid interest-only mortgages!

Buying a home is never a simple or easy process. It can be stressful, emotional, confusing, and outright exhausting. However, with the help of some basic financial rules, a great deal of the pressure and stress can be taken off of your shoulders. Remember:

- your home should not consume more than 22 percent of your TDSR
- choose an amortization period below 25 years
- save for a down payment outside of your retirement savings
- use the built-in benefits of a principle residence
- our expectations do not necessarily match our ability to pay

Following these simple guidelines will ensure that home owner-ship will complement your financial plan and not become the dreaded "money pit." With a better overall financial well-being, your home will be a source of pride and not a source of financial stress.

Chapter 7

The Joy of Living Debt Free:
Escaping the Third Assassin

I pay Visa with my MasterCard
—Bumper sticker (1)

When you run in debt, you give to another power over your Liberty.... The borrower is a Slave to the Lender, and the Debtor to the Creditor, disdain the Chain, preserve your freedom; and maintain your independency: Be industrious and free; be frugal and free.
—Benjamin Franklin, *Way to Wealth*

We no longer live in a society that encourages thriftiness, frugality, and financial prudence, but rather in one where wealth is primarily attained through perception and debt is the fuel. Ours is a world where many spend to belong and children learn to consume at an early age. Debt, probably the most powerful of the Money Assassins, exerts immense pressure, stress, and control over our lives. The stark reality is that debt and credit have become a normal and expected part of life. Debt has been so effective at forming part of our financial belief system that even the most astute, smart, and disciplined individuals have fallen prey to its persuasive and dangerous powers. To change these practices and mentalities and ultimately shake the weight of debt off of our backs, we must develop a different financial outlook on life, protect ourselves from our consumer culture and its trappings, and embrace voluntary constraints in our lives. In this chapter, we will explore some ways to eliminate our debt and avoid debt in the first place. In doing so, we can discover the joy of living debt free. But before we can hope to set ourselves free from the chains of debt, we must first reflect upon and decide who we are, what we stand for, and what we truly want and believe. This exploration of ourselves is quite possibly the best investment we will ever make.

Credit and debt fuel the perception of wealth, giving the illusion of social success, status, and wealth; however, underneath it all is great suffering. Acceptance and normalization of personal debt have done more to damage our financial well-being and freedom than any other factor. Since the 1970s, our society has gradually adopted personal debt as a fact and way of life. Many people are burdened with the invisible anxiety of carrying record levels of debt, working longer hours to finance their debt, and are financially stressed and isolated from help. When help is sought, most advice and would-be solutions to reduce and eliminate debt mistakenly focus on refinance strategies or debt education and ignore the need to reset our financial mindset. We need to put ourselves back to a time of life without debt in order to find more sustainable solutions to lifestyle and cash management.

The harmful effects of the burden of debt go largely unnoticed and untreated due to its invisible nature. When in serious debt, we are left feeling powerless and out of control. When we come to believe that we cannot alter our financial future, hopelessness sets in and we become unaware of and numb to the dangers of credit and debt dependency. (2) Although we most commonly associate problems with debt in financial terms, there are clearly other burdens, such as our valuable personal energy and overall wellness that are associated with carrying debt. Participants of one study identified debt as the number one factor that keeps their nose to the grindstone as well as the main barrier for those looking for a simpler life. (3) Fortunately, through the discovery of your life's intentions, financial creativity, adaptability, frugality, and overall awareness of the cost of convenience, you will see that there is an alternative way, a less energy-intensive way, and a less stressful way to live without debt. The ultimate goal for you is to become a "deadbeat"—don't worry, this is a good thing! *Deadbeat* is a term that lending institutions use to refer to people who regularly pay off their monthly credit balances. Becoming a "deadbeat" and living a life without debt is not an easy road given the nature of our consumer society, which is a society fuelled by a nation rooted in credit.

It is common for people with high levels of debt to feel ashamed or see themselves as failures, but this is misplaced and not a fair assessment. Although it is important that we assume some responsibility for our debt, we must also recognize the role that our economic environment and society's lack of awareness play in creating our debt. Given the mounting levels of debt and inability to see any solutions in sight, it is somewhat understandable why our fear of never regaining control drives us further and further away from the financial counselling we need. If and when advice is sought, it is often too late and is only done as a last resort. Unfortunately, bankruptcy is usually the common default option. Many people turn to credit counselling and bankruptcy firms. Today these firms are considered growth industries, as they are very profitable, yet they are not designed for financial rehabilitation. These organizations make their money through fees, refinancing, and bankruptcy, not by fixing the real problems: people spending beyond their means and practicing financially irresponsible lifestyles. After using these organizations, many people find themselves returning to a financial environment and system that was the problem in the first place.

To break free and escape from the shackles of debt, we must first rediscover and reconnect with both our financial convictions and values. The solutions to our problems are not found in learning more technical financial know-how such as paying high-interest debt first. It is important to understand that banks and other lending institutions, through debt products, earn billions of dollars and have a vested interest in ensuring that we continue to use these products, as they are obscenely profitable. Part of the problem in trying to eliminate our debt is that the process itself can be very emotional and time-consuming. Since most people have little time to spare, they feel they are unable to commit the time that may be required to eliminate their debt. Although the average working week is five days, the reality is that with interest rates on credit cards as high as 20 percent, after paying the interest on our debt, it is as if we are only working four days a week. (4) Many of us are already drained from using our energy just to keep up with the burden of maintaining our debt. Finding the time and energy to tackle our debt problems may appear too daunting of a task.

Jacob Needleman, author of *Money and the Meaning of Life*, asks his readers to imagine a prison where the prisoners do not know life outside the walls and spend all of their effort just to better the conditions inside their prison. This is similar to how many of us manage and service our debt. The idea of living without debt has become so foreign and obscure that we see no other way of living and turn, just like the prisoners, to efforts that will only better the conditions inside our financial prison instead of trying to escape from it. Banks and lending institutions serve as the wardens who prevent us from escaping. Their goal is to simply make the conditions bearable enough for us to stay and continue to participate. Home equity lines of credit, refinancing strategies, low-interest credit cards, credit surfing, free gifts, rate reductions on mortgages, discounts on store cards if you, sign up now, and, my favourite, reward programs are just a few examples of how credit organizations try to make our lives comfortable enough so that we keep playing the game. This is why debt and credit education are never about the elimination of your debt but rather about making your debt burden more manageable, effective, and comfortable.

One way our world of debt has been made more comfortable has been through the marketing of store and credit cards. The original purpose of stores such as Sears offering credit cards was to "generate greater retail sales and to reinforce customer loyalty, not to earn profit on finance charges." (1) Today's retailers are making substantial profits from financing and, in some cases, such as General Electric's, are actually generating higher profits from lending than from their core manufacturing divisions. With so much money on the line, it comes as no surprise that most of today's retail stores, such as Home Depot, IKEA, and HBC, have their own store credit cards. Manufacturing and retail giants such as General Electric, Sears, Ford, and others are now in the business of financing over 30 percent of all consumer credit. What began as a strategy to generate greater sales and strengthen customer loyalty has turned into a system of debt enslavement for millions of individuals. (1)

It was during the 1970s that consumers were first asked about how they felt about using credit cards and their attitudes towards them. The results showed that 75 percent of respondents said "that credit cards made it too easy to buy things that they may not really want or can't really afford" but stressed the main advantage of having a card is to be able to "buy without having the money." The author of the study, Lewis Mandell, was shocked to learn that 15 percent of wealthier families carried a balance and, not surprisingly, that the vast majority of all families fell prey to the temptation to buy more than was necessary. (1) One of the main reasons why credit cards have invested in reward or travel programs is to attract more affluent individuals. The use of credit cards by "deadbeats" creates the perception of widespread acceptance and prestige. Lenders also know that even if you are able to pay off your balance monthly, there will come a time when you forget or cannot pay, and the lender will be waiting. Unexpected things can happen, and a percentage of disciplined, financially astute individuals will fall on hard times and will need to finance a life transition. Rest assured, the lenders will be there, waiting and willing to lend us more than we need.

Credit card marketing campaigns mainly incorporate two themes in all of their advertisements: emotional spending and personal convenience. MasterCard hit a home run with emotional spending when they introduced their "priceless" series of commercials. These commercials have since been recognized as one of the most successful marketing campaigns ever. The commercials play on our heartstrings and give examples of how to provide "priceless" moments for loved ones, meanwhile ignoring the fact that it will cost you 20 percent of your life to pay for these moments! The second theme is personal convenience, a theme that is routinely emphasized through such slogans as "It's everywhere you want it to be" and "Don't leave home without it." (1) Convenience and emotional spending, as we have already seen, are robbers of financial freedom. In the hopes of breaking free from our burden of debt, it is imperative that we reduce or fully eliminate the use of credit cards from our consumptive behaviour and enjoy the benefits of being a "deadbeat"!

Life's Intentions

> *Knowing your purpose simplifies your life. It defines what you do*
> *and what you don't do. Your purpose becomes the standard you*
> *use to evaluate which activities are essential and which aren't.*
> —Rick Warren, *The Purpose Driven Life*

Maria Nemeth, psychologist and author of *The Energy of Money*, provides an excellent exercise to assist people in discovering their goals and destination in life. In her book, Nemeth describes the idea of life's intentions, a concept that helps us bring clarity and creativity to our direction in life and, in terms of our finances, helps establish some direction in our spending. In the words of Nemeth, "A life's intention…is a direction, aim or purpose that comes from deep within you. It's the living spirit behind your goals and dreams." (5) In knowing our life's intentions, we have a clear direction of where and how to focus our personal energy and spending. We are then at a much lower risk of being pulled off track by the agenda of friends, colleagues, or our consumer society and are better able to channel our financial resources towards our priorities, while reducing the temptation to incur unnecessary debt. I strongly encourage you to invest the time required to do this exercise, as the benefits are countless. As Nemeth states, "Life's intentions are your greatest personal treasure." In discovering or rediscovering your life's intentions, you will undoubtedly watch your financial opportunities expand, as you will save thousands of dollars by avoiding the wrong path. Let us begin.

Step one: You will need a minimum of 40 minutes in a quiet place where you will be uninterrupted. Bring a notebook or a couple of pieces of paper and pen with you. If you want, you can work in two 20-minute segments, but just make sure to give yourself plenty of time to do the exercise.

Step two: Begin by taking a few minutes to relax to help clear your mind. Now pretend you have found a magic lamp. There is a magic genie in the lamp who will give you anything you want. There are no limits or restrictions in terms of money, time, or talent. For example, I am less than six feet tall and unable to shoot a three-pointer if my life depended on it, yet I could request to play in the NBA. You may also make a request that is pure fantasy, such as being able to fly or float around the world. On your blank piece of paper, write a list of *everything that you have ever wanted to do or have in life.* Be sure to write everything that is on your mind on the paper. There is no such thing as a silly or outrageous request, as this is a private list only for you.

Some examples could be owning a home, owning a cabin, learning to scuba dive, becoming a fish, travelling to Italy, taking the kids to Disneyland, raising a million dollars for your favourite charity, owning your own business, becoming a teacher, running a marathon, going to outer space, writing a book, etc. As you can see, your list can go on and on. Make sure to give yourself an adequate amount of time because once you begin, numerous ideas and goals will pop into your mind. You need to take the time to reflect on your list of requests—trust me, it's worth it!

Step three: Look at each item on your list and ask yourself, "Why do I want this? What desire will it satisfy?" When you discover the underlying reason, make sure to write it down on a separate piece of paper. Put the answers (the underlying reasons) in the form of "to be…." Nemeth uses the following example. Goal = Want to take my kids to Disneyland. Reason = To satisfy the desire to be a good parent. In this case, then, you would write, "To be a good parent." Another goal might be, "I would like to travel to China or India." Reason = To satisfy my desire for adventure. You would therefore write, "To be adventurous." It's alright if you have a "to be" that is repeated or comes up often, such as "to be a good friend, parent, or successful." Other examples of "to be…" might include "secure," "comfortable," "accomplished," "a good parent," "an inspiration," "caring or giving," to name but a few.

You should now have a list of everything you have ever wanted to do or have, as well as the accompanying "to be" list. At this point, you may notice that many of your reasons "to be…" will be duplicates. Take note of which ones are repeated. In taking the time to make up my personal list, I realized that in order to fulfill my "to be..." list I did not necessarily have to acquire what was on my first list of wants. In fact, there were multiple ways of accomplishing my life's intentions, many of which did not require very much money! For example, my list demonstrated my desire for adventure. Yet, although I wanted to be adventurous, I realized that I did not have to go to China to find adventure, as I could go hiking in the mountains or go whitewater canoeing in Northern Saskatchewan. One of my most memorable family vacations was the time we had, according to my dad, "A Poor Man's Hawaii." Being an avid skiing family and living in Saskatoon meant annual ski trips to the mountains. However, one year we did not have the money to go and instead went skiing at the local ski hill called Mount Blackstrap, better known as the "Pimple on the Prairies." Along with friends, our family went skiing for the day, booked a hotel back in the city that had waterslides, ordered pizza, and watched movies. It was a memorable weekend filled with friends, relaxation, and skiing. It also cost a fraction of the price of going to the mountains for a ski trip. I am certainly not saying that you should never leave your home to go on a holiday; I am only trying to provide an example of how a little creativity can go a long way in offering us fulfillment and enjoyment in our lives without having to incur debt.

This exercise serves as an excellent tool in helping to reveal alternative ways for us to accomplish our life's intentions without having to spend a lot of money or accumulate debt. It also highlights how we are caught up in a culture that has planted ideas and expectations about the way we should live. Deep down we know that we do not need to take our children to Disneyland to be good parents, nor do we need to earn a six-figure salary to be a good spouse. If we are ever to break free from the shackles of debt, we must learn to be open to alternative ways to accomplish our life's intentions that fit within our financial means. Your life's intentions are a powerful list of personal motivators; put your list in a place where you can see it on a daily basis or carry it inside your wallet or purse as a checkpoint. This will allow you to reflect on your values and priorities before you purchase anything. This safeguard of sorts will ensure that you spend your hard-earned money in alignment with *your* values and priorities and not those of the marketers or consumer society. Recognizing that your life's intentions will undoubtedly change throughout the course of your life, I would recommend that you revisit them every three to five years.

Here are some examples of a person's dreams and what they can mean:

"Want to have, do, or be"	"to be…"
Cabin	to be…comfortable and relaxed
Porsche	to be…successful
Million dollars	to be…worry free
Fly like a bird	to be…free
Travel to India	to be…adventurous, educated, and worldly
Go camping with my family	to be…a good parent
To lose weight or get back in shape	to be…a healthy, vibrant, and energized

Embracing Constraints

An essential ingredient in the fight to eliminate debt is the need to embrace both discipline and voluntary constraints in our daily lives to help keep us on the path to financial well-being. In his book, *The Paradox of Choice*, Professor Barry Schwartz suggests that our society would be better off if we embraced voluntary constraints on our freedom of choice. Schwartz lists five ways that this can be accomplished:

1) If we embrace certain voluntary constraints on freedom of choice
2) If we seek "good enough" instead of the best
3) If we lower our expectations about the results of our decisions
4) If our decisions were nonreversible
5) If we paid less attention to what others around us were doing. (6)

Perhaps the easiest way of introducing a voluntary constraint into your financial plan is by using cash more often. A common recurring theme throughout the course of this book is the peril of plastic in our lives. We have already explored in detail how credit and debit cards are one of the largest culprits in debt accumulation. We have also seen how plastic has become a common payment method, as it allows us to basically have an unlimited amount of cash available at any time, anywhere. Restricting your use of this payment method will save you from making hundreds if not thousands of unnecessary and unwanted purchases. The use of cash as a payment method gives you an immediate tally of your financial "budget" and automatically forces you to think twice before handing over your hard-earned money. This example of a voluntary constraint clearly reveals the financial benefit in restricting ourselves, as the decision to do so will likely reduce your current spending by approximately 25 percent. Most important of all, you won't even notice a difference in terms of lifestyle satisfaction, as you are only cutting out the "wasteful" spending, not the necessities of life or the luxuries that you truly want.

One of my favourite quotations from business philosopher/ motivational speaker Jim Rohn: "Discipline is a small price to pay compared to the weight of regret and disappointment." This best sums up the concept of embracing voluntary constraints. Whereas many cast the term *constraint* in a negative light, voluntarily choosing to embrace financial constraints in our lives may be one of the most positive things we can do for ourselves. Indeed, through discipline and embracing such constraints, you will be more empowered to achieve some of your greatest financial dreams, be it early retirement, sending your child to college or university, living debt free, or having the financial stability to change careers. Too many of us have regret in our lives. Let discipline and constraint shield you from the marketing industry and the pressures of our consumer society while embracing your newfound freedom to live a life without financial regret and disappointment.

In Search of "Good Enough"

> *Our rising expectations have outstripped our incomes, leaving the*
> *average consumer-patriot increasingly in debt.*
> —Joe Dominguez and Vicki Robin, *Your Money or Your Life*

At the heart of our addiction to and dependency on debt is the reality that our lifestyle and consumer expectations no longer match our incomes. Our unrealistic expectations have risen to such new heights that in order to achieve our perceived needs and expectations, we are required to look to debt to fill the widening crack between needs and wants. If we are ever to stop our slide down this slippery slope of financial indebtedness, we must come to accept the idea of "enough." We must change our attitudes about possessions, money, and financial success. It is imperative that we answer the following question, as it will serve as a lifelong financial marker: "How do I know when I have enough possessions, experiences, and money?"

According to *The Chinese Book of Wisdom*, "He who knows he has enough is rich." (4) I believe this is an excellent perspective on wealth, as it puts control in the hands of people and not in those of bankers, investment managers, marketers, and stock markets. This perspective on wealth makes room for many other things in our lives that might make us wealthy aside from money, such as family, friends, health, and other aspects of well-being. In the *The Pursuit of Happiness*, David Myers writes that the "river of happiness is fed far less by wealth than by the streams of ordinary pleasures." (7) These daily pleasures include cooking, friends, storytelling, fishing, sports, music, and books. Fortunately, even during difficult times, "one never has to look far to see the campfires of gentle (and happy) people." (7)

In a world where we are constantly told that we never have enough, it comes as no surprise that we struggle to know when we have "enough." The danger in living in this world is that we are never satisfied with what we have and we are constantly longing for more. To regain our financial well-being, it is crucial that we have a financial goal so that we may know when enough is enough. As a step towards discovering this financial "end point," I encourage you to sit down and write on a piece of paper an amount of money that constitutes "enough" for you. In knowing what it is you want, you are empowered to step away from the game of "relativism roulette" that is jeopardizing the financial well-being of millions of people. You will always be surrounded by others who have more and businesses that will tempt you to crave more. With a goal in mind, you are already able to step off of the financial treadmill that is leading many astray, as you will no longer be chasing an abstract idea, but rather will be placing yourself along the path to your financial freedom.

While the benefits of undertaking such an exercise are clear, the reality is that some people are scared to discover this number, as they are afraid that they will be lost once they reach this goal and won't know what to do with themselves once they've achieved their target. Don't be afraid. I assure you that you will discover that "enough" is a fearless place, a place that is full of alertness, creativity, and freedom. It is also a place where you will be able to fully enjoy and appreciate the joys that money can add to your life. Once you have located a place where enough is enough, you will be free to release and launch yourself toward other aspects of your life that are beyond financial goals. Everyone will have their own individualized standard or place of "enough," a standard or place that will change throughout your life. Your job is to always be aware of your goal, by focusing on the target that you have set for yourself. If you can sum up the courage to do so, I would also encourage you to talk to your friends, family, and colleagues and come up with some ideas about what constitutes "enough" in your lives, in terms of work, love, health, and money.

If you apply the concept of "good enough" to your everyday buying habits, you will save hundreds if not thousands of dollars per year. When you adopt a lifestyle that subscribes to the idea of "good enough," you are essentially placing control back in your hands and guaranteeing yourself increased savings that are risk free. (4) Be grateful and content with the possessions you already have. Before you buy something new, ask yourself if you already have something that fits and matches your needs. When purchasing vehicles, homes, vacations, clothing, and toys, ensure that you find the things that are "good enough" and that meet your needs. Don't get trapped into the world of "best or better." As we discussed in "Spending to Belong and the New Necessities," it is important that we focus on our goals and that we do not pay attention to the behaviours of others. We must avoid trying to emulate the fictitious and harmful lifestyles we see on TV, in movies, and on the Internet. Ultimately, we must remember that we are not trying to keep up with "The Jetsons" or the "techno-Joneses" but are instead trying to keep up with our own financial plan that is in line with our values, goals, and financial reality.

The Cost of Convenience

To eliminate debt from our lives and achieve financial well-being, it is vital that we understand the "cost of convenience." Convenience is one of the most expensive everyday expenditures we incur. We will briefly touch on four of the most common areas of convenience: food, communication, transportation, and payment methods.

When it comes to eating, we all have to do it and there is no way of getting around it. Yet the food costs we incur do not have to be as high as they are. One of the reasons for the increase in eating out is that many of us are losing the skill of cooking. Instead we have chosen the fast-paced lifestyle of having others, who do not have the interest of our health at heart, grow, raise, prepare, and cook our food. Pre-packaged foods are often bad for our health and the environment and extremely expensive compared to growing and making our own food. Eating out has become the default for feeding ourselves because we no longer make the time to prepare and cook our own meals. Eating out prevents us from allocating hundreds of dollars a month to our financial plan, not to mention the resulting health consequences from our poor eating habits. I recommend that you track your food spending and ask yourself the question, "Are the costs to my health and financial plan really worth the price?" Some might answer yes and choose other areas in their lives to cut back, while others might be shocked at how much is being spent on food and might change their habits and possibly even rediscover the joys of growing and cooking their own food!

There is no doubt of the need to communicate with others in our communities and beyond. To what extent though does this communication have to be instantaneous? If you add up the cost of your cell phone, home phone, and Internet, this instant ability to communicate may cost you thousands of dollars over the course of your life. For example, take an average Canadian household and calculate their respective Internet, home, and cell phone expenditures. Using Statistics Canada's figures, the cost would be approximately $120 per month. Note that these costs only include the monthly billing and not the hardware upgrades or the purchase of a new cell phone that happens, on average, every 18 months. If you could reduce that number by half over a 40-year period and save the difference in an RRSP at 6.5 percent, you would have an extra $150,000 at retirement! Again, these figures use Canadian averages that include those households without cell phones and Internet, suggesting that expenses and potential savings are significantly higher. The question we need to ask ourselves is, "Is instant and immediate communication worth two to four years of one's working life?"

In the chapter "Living Car-Lite" we took a look at the most expensive convenience in our life: transportation. Transportation, an essential and constant need in our lives, is a key player in determining our financial well-being. At the risk of repeating myself in this chapter, I will only highlight one important figure: that on average, approximately 20 percent of one's total income is consumed though the use of our vehicles. As we have seen, our transportation needs are one of the first and most essential areas to examine if we hope to eliminate debt and create wealth.

The cost of convenience is also found in our methods of payment, a concept that was already discussed in the "First Assassin." The convenience of debit and credit cards as preferred payment methods constitute a sizable share of our unnecessary and often regretful spending. Because payment methods are such a large culprit in spending beyond our means, it is important that we remember the need to reduce our use of both credit and debit cards. The convenience of plastic can cost us, through the impulsive purchases we make with these cards.

There is no doubt that there are situations when paying for the cost of convenience is worth the price and times when it is okay to indulge. In highlighting a few of the conveniences in our lives and their associated costs, I am trying to shed light on the role that they play in our financial well-being. My advice to readers is not to avoid these conveniences altogether, but instead to develop a keen sense of *awareness* of the depth of the costs we incur in using these conveniences. I encourage you to ask yourself how you might reduce your expenditures and prioritize the conveniences in your life.

The F Word: Frugality

Each year, we incur hundreds of dollars of personal debt through small unwanted or unnecessary purchases. If we are to live debt free, we need to adopt frugality into our lifestyle and financial mindset. Unfortunately, frugality gets a bad rap as it is commonly associated with cheapness. Although the term often conjures up images of Scrooge counting his pennies, frugality is not about hoarding but rather about maximizing your spending gratification. The biggest benefit in embracing frugality having a financial guardian with you 24 hours a day, seven days a week. The frugal financial mindset provides a checkpoint that awakens your financial conscience just long enough, perhaps a split second, for you to avoid unwanted, unnecessary, and expensive impulse purchases that lead to more debt and regret. Frugality creates space in your financial life to give; it is the gateway to generosity because frugal people spend their money in alignment with their values. A frugal lifestyle ensures that individuals and families have money to allocate towards what is truly important to them, enabling them to be generous with their time and money. While many might cringe at the thought of being labelled frugal, or espousing a lifestyle of frugality, the goal of adopting frugality in your life is not to force you to cut corners around your expenses or prevent you from ever taking out your wallet, but is instead to enable you to establish a sense of "good enough" in your life, while perhaps subscribing more to a level of "frugal comfort." (8)

The Good Debt Myth

Debt management is very similar to weight management. If you ask most personal trainers and dieticians to tell you the key to losing weight, they will say that you simply need to expend more calories than you consume, end of story. It doesn't matter if you only eat the healthiest of foods, if you consume more calories than your body burns, you will gain weight. The same reality applies to debt—too many "good debt purchases" will be a weight on your finances.

You may have heard of the idea that there is "good debt" and "bad debt." Good debt is described as any debt incurred for the purpose of acquiring an asset that will either generate income or appreciate in value. Some examples are student loans, which eventually lead to increased opportunities for higher income and greater job satisfaction, and mortgages, which enable us to participate in the real estate market. Assets purchased with bad debt provide no returns to the borrower and cost them more money in the long run. Buying a new pair of jeans or eating out at a restaurant and charging the bill to your credit card are examples of bad debt. Vehicles are another common example cited as bad debt. These examples seem rather logical. Investing in education and assets that build wealth are good, yet caution is required, as there are two important points that are regularly overlooked and ignored.

The first point that is often overlooked is that, as in the case of calories and weight loss, the type of debt you carry will not determine your financial well-being, rather, your financial well-being will be determined by how much debt you carry. If you go out and buy a home (good debt) and spend beyond your means in doing so, you will struggle to save and be "cash strapped." On the other hand, as is the case with bad calories, bad debt need not be harmful to your financial well-being if it is within acceptable parameters.

My advice regarding debt is that you try and focus on managing your total debt service ratio (TDSR). Given that many people have TDSRs that often consume 30–40 percent of their income, the ratio is clearly a prime target to free up cash flow for other priorities. I would suggest that you strive to maintain a TDSR between 20 and 25 percent, and rarely or never go beyond 30 percent. By reducing your TDSR by 10–15 percent, you will free up hundreds of dollars, in some cases thousands of dollars, per month that can be allocated towards debt elimination and your financial plan. It is important that you focus on the root of the problem when managing your TDSR—the amount of debt that you have relative to your income. At the end of the day, this is ultimately all that matters to your financial well-being. However, rearranging and organizing your lifestyle to fit into a TDSR of 20–25 percent will not be easy. For some it may require changing homes, delaying the purchase of a home, or buying a different vehicle.

The second aspect of good debt that is overlooked is its tendency to become a gateway or catalyst to bad debt. Post-secondary institutions are a perfect environment for the credit card industry to target one of their most profitable markets: students. (1) On average, students carry more cards and larger balances than the general population. This has helped lead to a situation in which the majority of students find themselves behind the financial eight ball before they even begin their careers. (1) The average debt load of a graduating student from university is $19,500, with the majority of the debt resulting from tuition and books, and approximately $5,000 resulting from lifestyle and "survival." The use of credit usually begins as a "survival" or temporary strategy, a logical and sensible way of paying the bills. However, the problem lies in the fact that this casual use is often how many addictions begin, such as with alcohol and drug addiction. Many students develop an addiction to credit at college and university. This comes as no surprise when you consider the many purchases that these students often make: laptops, spring break trips to Mexico, ski trips to the mountains, lunches, dinners, clothes, and don't forget drinks! The easy access to money for a demographic that has been groomed to consume and the belief that their debts will be easily repaid once they begin working is a lethal financial combination. Although I strongly support and believe in the value of post-secondary education, I also feel that students need to be aware that life at university or college is laced with an endless parade of spending opportunities. If students are not careful, they can find themselves quickly and subtly acquiring large sums of "bad debt" that they will not be able to pay off as quickly as they acquired it. Most important of all is the fact that these bad financial habits are hard to break and may begin to erode any financial foundation.

The need to avoid debt and develop good financial habits at an early age has also been addressed throughout the course of this book. When you acquire debt at an early stage of your life, you significantly reduce your options and make it very difficult to choose a simpler life. Part of the reason many youths fall into the debt trap is that they are specifically targeted by lending institutions. These institutions try and give them a "taste for credit" and a glimpse into what an upper-class lifestyle is like. Credit card companies seek out high-school and post-secondary students, as they are an extremely profitable market. The current level of debt owed by post-secondary students in Canada when they have been granted a loan by a government source is approximately $20,000 per student. However, when money is also owed to a non-governmental source, Canadian student debt explodes to over $32,000 for money owed on credit cards and personal lines of credit. (10, 11) Credit institutions have a vested interest in creating credit dependency at a young age—the younger the customer is, the easier it is to establish a belief system where credit is not only accepted, but an expected part of life. For example, MasterCard has teamed up with MuchMusic, an extremely popular music channel, to expose children 13 years or older to credit cards and help shape their plastic-friendly purchasing behaviour at a young age. The slogan of the card is "Free Yourself"—break free from parents and "get all the purchasing freedom you need anytime you want" without having to ask permission. The advertisement states, "It looks like a credit card, but it's not." (12) By getting used to the idea of using a credit card at an early age, MasterCard is essentially setting the stage for a lifetime of uphill financial battles for these teenagers.

"To Save or to Pay off Debt: That is the Question"

One of the most common questions people have is whether to save or reduce their debt. Intuitively and theoretically the answer seems obvious: pay off your debt. However, what works in theory does not always work in practice. In theory, it makes a lot of sense to pay off high-interest credit card debt first. It is therefore understandable why many people choose to work towards reducing their debt instead of trying to increase their savings. Yet the reality of this strategy is that many are left with increased debt while being no further ahead in their savings. This usually occurs because often we do not address the core issue of our debt problem: lifestyle dependency on debt.

The following example of a common debt cycle will help to explain the above phenomenon: You go to school and graduate with student loans and no savings. You then get a job and need a vehicle. You now have a car loan and continue to spend on furniture, vacations, entertainment, a computer, and some "new necessities." Meanwhile, your credit card bill continues to grow. Amongst all of these financial obligations, the unexpected happens: your vehicle breaks down and you have to come up with $1,500 to fix it. Since you have no available cash or savings to dip into, you put the payment on your line of credit. This example shows how we have become accustomed to debt and how we expect it as a part of life. Our inability to develop a cash safety net leaves debt as the only option for future emergency and life events. We are left with few options. The following example illustrates how we are self-empowered when we have options and choices.

Person A: Has no savings and no debt = Net Worth $0.00

Person B: Has $5,000 in savings and $5,000 in debt =
Net Worth $0.00

As you can see in the above example, individuals A and B both have a net worth of zero. However, there is a subtle difference between the two. When faced with an unexpected expense of, let's say, $1,000, Person B has an option while Person A does not. Person B is in a position of choice. This individual may either incur an extra $1,000 of debt or reduce their savings by $1,000. When people have options, they feel a degree of control over their future. Options also reinforce positive financial habits and allow us to continue to save. Person A, on the other hand, has no choice and must therefore incur debt to cover the $1,000 expense. There is nothing more disheartening than getting an unexpected bill thrown at you that puts you back into debt after battling all year to get your debt down to zero. Knowing how hard it was to eliminate debt the first time around, the thought of doing it again may lead you to adopt the idea that maybe "debt is just a part of life."

I believe that it is important that you do both—save your money and reduce your debt at the same time—and there are three important reasons why you should do so. First, the positive psychological benefit of doing what you know you should be doing—saving—is great positive reinforcement. Just being in the habit of saving regularly, regardless of the amount, will make you feel positive and hopeful about your financial future. Second, by establishing early habits of savings, you will be able to take advantage of numerous long-term financial benefits. Finally, when you have options, you regain financial control and feel empowered as a result. For example, if you are paying $300 per month in debt payments, consider putting $50 in a savings account that you cannot access and $250 towards your debt. What often happens is that people find the extra $50 elsewhere, perhaps through a change in lifestyle, and continue to pay the $300. Not only does this strategy help people pay off their debt more quickly, it also instills in them solid financial habits that lead to financial well-being and the belief that debt does not have to be a part of life.

The path to becoming debt free is not a smooth or trouble-free road. It can be full of bumps and detours that require effort and creativity on our part. To achieve our end goal of living without debt, we must adopt alternative lifestyle and consumption habits, develop an awareness of today's economic trappings, embrace voluntary financial constraint, and, most important of all, summon up the courage to live in keeping with our real values. Although the path may not be easy, you will begin to discover the joy of living debt free when you make the decision to no longer accept debt as a part of life.

Chapter 8

Financial Wisdom

Aggressive savings outperform great investments

As a financial planner, I strive to provide my clients with as many options as possible and I always tell them that as their planner it is my job to ensure that whenever they call I have good news for them— news that puts them in a financial position of choice and control. If they are sick, I want to make sure that they have enough money to take the time to recover without being burdened by financial worries or concerns. If they lose their job or want to change their career, it is important that they have the financial resources to allow them to take the time to make the transition. If a great opportunity comes along, I want them to have the money to take advantage of it. If they want to retire, I want them to be able to. If they find their dream home, I want them to be able to afford it. If there is an unexpected death in the family, it is my job to ensure that the family is left in a position of financial dignity. If they want their kids to be able to attend a post-secondary institution, I want money to be available for them to do so. While many of these events are predictable and foreseeable and can therefore be planned for in advance, some are completely beyond and out of our control. Our inability to predict financial hardships that may affect us highlights the need to develop a proper and comprehensive financial plan that incorporates strategies for both the financial accumulation of assets as well as the protection of these assets.

Many of those who have had financial success were often given a piece of advice, took it to heart, and incorporated this advice into their financial plan throughout the course of their lives. Early in my career, I was fortunate to come across such advice. "Save a year's worth of your income in cash and you will be able to take advantage of life-changing opportunities and survive financial emergencies." For most people, this bit of advice seems like a daunting and impossible task, but as we have explored throughout this book, our ability to save largely depends on managing our total debt service ratio (TDSR). Although my wife and I never quite made it to saving a year's worth of income, this advice has nevertheless served us to get on the right track and save a significant amount. We have reaped the rewards of making an effort to save and I can now speak from personal experience about the value of maintaining a low TDSR. My wife and I were both able to make career changes that were financially stress-free; we had minimal financial stress when a costly, unexpected home repair was required; and we also had access to cash to be able to afford an extremely important event in our lives. We were only able to afford these costs because of our commitment to maintaining a low TDSR. I am hopeful that you have already discovered some sound pieces of advice in the previous chapters and that you will find a few more revealed in this one.

To get the most out of this chapter, a little participation is required. Throughout the chapter, you will be asked to do some financial calculations. These calculations can be completed on the *Money Assassins* website at *www.moneyassassins.com*. Follow the "Individuals" link and click on the "Financial Calculations" section to do the math. Depending on where you are on your financial journey, some sections and pieces of information will be more important or interesting than others. However, I would encourage readers to look in all areas to discover ways of improvement, since the creation and protection of wealth requires a holistic approach. Having said that, there are three sections I would ask readers to pay special attention to. The first is the "Investor/Saver Confusion," as it will bring clarity to the confusion surrounding saving and investing and will provide a unique and important perspective on investing. The second is the "World of Personal Insurance," a largely misunderstood area of personal finance that can prove invaluable, and if ignored, can be financially crippling. Last, but certainly not least, is the "Heart Attack Graph," where we will now turn our attention. We begin our examination of some of these pearls of financial wisdom with this section, as I believe it to be the backbone and most important part of any financial plan.

The Heart Attack Graph

There are no known associated health risks with financial planning except for possibly one. It is what I call the "Heart Attack Graph." The Heart Attack Graph got its name from the reactions that I often get from my clients when they realize how much they needed to contribute to their financial plan. A common myth is that you only need to save 10 percent of your gross income. The truth is that it is more like 20–30 percent of your before tax income that you should be saving. Before you complete your own graph, remember that the graph is a guide and tool to help you get to where you want to go. Most people have never looked at their cash flow and taken this step, so congratulations on making it this far and don't forget to breathe!

Looking in the mirror and taking an honest look at your finances can be one of the scariest, most stressful and nerve-racking processes you will ever experience. While some say that "ignorance is bliss," when it comes to your financial future, ignorance can cost you a lot of time and money. Individual behaviour plays the biggest role in the accumulation of wealth, and it is important to realize that your financial behaviour is probably the most important step in the whole planning process. It is important that you do not get stressed over this process, as you will likely find that you are probably saving more today than you think. Summon the courage, get on your computer, and go to *www.moneyassassins.com.* Click on the link for "Individuals" and then click on "Heart Attack Graph." Take an honest look at your financial cash flow—you will be glad that you did.

A financial plan should be designed to make a difference in your life. To achieve a level of financial significance for you and your family, I recommend striving to commit 20–30 percent of your *before tax income* towards your financial plan. This will be a big number for those who have done little to no planning, but don't be afraid. By following many of the recommendations throughout the book, you will be able to free up the necessary cash flow to commit to your financial plan. At first it will be common for many readers to find that their current life circumstances and commitments will make this target difficult or possibly even out of reach. What is important is that you start. Do something—begin with a minimum commitment of 15 percent. Allocating anything less than 15 percent of your gross income will lead to false hope and disappointment. If you wish to enjoy the benefits of a stress free and debt free financial life, it is important to have the intent and commitment to work and structure your life and expenses around the 20–30 percent commitment target.

The first part of the Heart Attack Graph tallies all of your contributions for your financial plan, separating them between the accumulation and protection portions. The second part demonstrates how much you need to contribute to achieve the 20 or 30 percent levels. The *Money Assassins* website will guide you through the process. All deposits, payments, and commitments that you are contributing to your financial goals should be accounted for, including personal insurance. Remember that financial planning is more art than science, so as a rough guideline, 80–85 percent of your money should be allocated towards the accumulation portion, the fun, sexy side of your plan! This can include retirement and pension savings, short- and medium-term investments, as well as any other cash accumulation savings, including government savings bonds or high-interest savings accounts. This leaves approximately 15–20 percent to be allocated towards the protection side of your financial plan.

Financial planning is no different from the oft-used statement in the world of sports that "defense wins championships." As many people are surely aware, life can throw us a curveball at any time. It is prudent to ensure that you have designed a "defensive" financial strategy to help withstand these unforeseen and unplanned events, as they have the potential to jeopardize your economic status and security. Such events might include the loss of your job, sickness, injury, or death; all have the potential to have severe financial consequences. On a risk matrix, the probability of such events range from low to probable, but the potential financial severity of these events is high. For the few dollars a month that is required, you will be able to eliminate these financial risks. Protection should be a part of all financial budgets.

The percentage split and allocation between the accumulation and protection sides of your plan may be higher or lower depending on your personal circumstances. If you are self-employed you may need to allocate a higher amount towards disability insurance compared to someone who has a group disability plan. It is also common that the protection portion of your plan will represent a higher percentage of your plan when you are younger. The primary reason for this is that you have a longer time period to insure and protect. Another reason is that your income is usually lower when you are younger compared to the later part of your career when you will have more disposable income to save. As your income grows, the percentage that is allocated towards the protection side will decrease and more will be allocated to the "fun stuff"—the accumulation side! For those who have permanent life insurance and a savings component included, such as universal life or a participating policy, the amount that is being contributed to the savings part of the plan can be included on the accumulation side and the cost of the insurance portion can be added to the protection side. This will give a fair account of your plan's overall allocation. But as a general guideline, if you are allocating more than 20 percent of your financial plan's money towards protection and insurance, then you might be overprotecting or over insuring yourself, but everyone has varying levels of comfort and one should talk to an insurance professional to ensure they have the appropriate coverage for their specific circumstances. To gain the right balance between the protection and accumulation portions of your plan, you should seek advice from a certified financial planner or insurance professional.

Here is an example of a financial plan cash flow analysis for a household income (aged 30) of $100,000:

$100,000 household income: 20 percent financial plan = $20,000 ($1,660 per month)

Accumulation		Protection	
Retirement savings	$500	Life Insurance	$150
Pension	$700	Disability Insurance	$60
Non-Registered Savings	$200	Critical Illness Coverage	$50

This allocation gives a rough break down of 85 percent accumulation and 15 percent protection.

Emergency/Opportunity Fund

Maintaining a sufficient cash reserve should be an essential part of your financial plan and should be one of the first financial goals you strive to achieve. Having access to cash allows you to deal with sudden emergencies with less stress and permits you to take advantage of opportunities. Here is an interesting exercise: Think of an amount of money that you would be comfortable with knowing you could access and have in your hands within three days (lines of credit, credit cards, and other forms of debt do not count). Write it down here—don't worry, there are no wrong answers:_____.

The amount of money you choose to have on reserve will differ from other people because of personal circumstances and priorities. · Many people may have heard that it is wise to have three months' of income saved, but the reality is that 75 percent of Canadians have not achieved this level. Given that three months of your income represents 25 percent of your annual income, it is a stretch to expect people to go from having 0 percent of their annual income saved to 25 percent. I believe that the first step is to have a minimum of 10 percent of your annual household income in accessible cash and to strive to attain 20 percent within ten years. Begin by saving 2.5 percent of your monthly, before tax, household income. This will allow you to achieve the 10 percent goal within four years and reach the 20 percent target before year ten. Remember that this is money that you will likely spend in the short-term either on opportunities or in addressing emergencies. This money is not being set aside for twenty years into the future. This money is being placed out of reach of the Money Assassins and is readily available for you to spend in alignment with your life's intentions and priorities. Go to *www.moneyassassins.com* for help to calculate your emergency fund saving numbers. Place these savings into a high-interest savings account or a low-risk mutual fund, such as a money market fund. The key to making this work is that you cannot have easy access to this account and it must not be accessible through your bank card. Set up your emergency savings account so that you have to make a phone call or complete a form to access the money. This extra effort to access your money acts like a built-in financial guard against impulse spending and awakens your financial conscience to ensure that this spending is in line with your financial values and goals.

Today, individuals have access to lines of credit or home equity lines of credit ranging from $10,000 to hundreds of thousands of dollars. Many people have mistakenly come to believe that these lines of credit are in fact their money. Relying on this debt to cover financial emergencies and opportunities, many people have confused *access* to money with *ownership* of it. Lines of credit have given many a false sense of security. I cannot stress it enough: *money from a line of credit is not yours!* Instead of having your own savings earn at least 3 percent, many of us borrow money at 6 percent. That is a 9 percent swing in the wrong direction. Lines of credit do not give you control over your life but rather give the lender control over you. It is crucial that you realize that lines of credit are good for lenders, not individuals. Lines of credit should not be seen as financial emergency funds and should not be used as such. As I have stressed throughout the book, when you are financially successful, you are in a position of power and have options that allow you to control the decisions you make.

Saving for a Down Payment

The key to being able to make a down payment on a home, as is the case with most financial planning, is to start early. Good financial planning results in an abundance of options and choices for the individual. Although home ownership may or may not be one of your financial goals at the moment, most individuals would agree that if

the situation or certain circumstances were to change, given the opportunity, they would like to be in a position of control and have the
option to buy. When it comes to buying a home, many clients often
say that they are "just looking around" or that they want to buy
"maybe one or two years down the road," and within months I receive a call telling me that they have just put in an offer. The timing
of when you will purchase a home is often unknown and is dependent upon a variety of factors, such as your career, getting a good deal,
the status of a relationship, or a number of other possible major life
events. The goal or objective of saving for a down payment should
be security and liquidity, easy access rather than growth. If your down
payment savings are in risky investments and they suddenly drop just
when your dream home comes on the market, you will lose. For example, if you had $20,000 and your investments dropped 10 percent,
your down payment account would now be $18,000—not the time
to have to liquidate your investments. Put your down payment savings
into a very conservative portfolio and if your time horizon for purchasing a home is under one year, put your money into a high-interest
savings account or money market fund.

At the time of writing, the Canadian government is moving forward to allow Canadians to save $5,000 per year in a Tax Free Savings
Account (TFSA) in the 2009 tax year. This means that there would
be no tax on any investment gains or withdrawals from this type of
account. A TFSA will be a great place to begin saving for a down
payment.

The following are three quick points regarding the down payment on a home:

1) Most individuals cannot afford the 25% down payment to
avoid the Canadian Mortgage and Housing Corporation (CMHC)
fees, but make sure that you put some money down nonetheless.
Avoid a 0 percent down payment, as you will end up paying significantly more through additional fees.

2) Don't use all of your cash for a down payment. Keep some
money on hand for emergencies, or debt will be your only option
when unexpected home expenses pop up.

3) If you do not own a home, begin building a down payment

savings account to give you options when the opportunity to buy arises.

RRSPs Are Great...but Don't Overcommit

One of the first financial decisions that most Canadians make is to open a Registered Retirement Savings Plan (RRSP). Two of the most appealing features of RRSPs are the tax deductibility of the contributions and the tax deferment of the investment growth. RRSPs are designed as a long-term planning tool, yet most rush into them, overcommitting their cash flow only to have to access the money years before retirement to pay for unplanned things and un-expected bills. While the financial services industry has done a good job of promoting RRSPs and the need to start them early, the same cannot be said of the industry's success in overall financial planning. On the one hand, the industry has promoted RRSP savings to young individuals, while on the other it has failed to prepare them for life.

Yes, RRSPs are great, and it is wise to begin investing your money early on; however, we must also recognize that throughout the course of our lives, there will be many other events that will require cash be-fore we retire. Before the age of 30, it is common for people to have to repay loans, buy a vehicle, possibly move to a new city, buy a home, buy furniture, travel, date, get married, have children, and hopefully have some fun on the side! Ultimately, you should save and put money into RRSPs, but make sure that you reduce your contributions, not your overall financial commitment, and ensure that you have built an ample cash reserve. For example, if you are putting $200 in your RRSP and have nothing saved for opportunities or emergencies, you may find yourself in trouble. Think of your RRSP as a one-way street: money goes in but cannot come out. Savings accounts give you much more flexibility because if you over save, you always have the option of depositing any extra money into your RRSP at a later date with no penalties. Penalties can arise, however, if you withdraw money early from your RRSP (before you retire), as tax will have to be paid on the amount withdrawn. Worst of all is that you will lose that RRSP contribution room forever.

The Investor/Saver Confusion

Since the late 1970s and early '80s, the financial services and mutual fund industries have played an important role in confusing the public by implying that we are a nation of investors when in fact we are a nation of lost savers. Investing has been marketed as the smart, savvy means to reach financial prosperity. The saver is seen as dull, overly cautious, and outdated. Individuals, especially younger people, have been misguided, largely by the financial services industry and finance books, into believing that investment returns will provide for an early retirement and financial prosperity.

Allow me to pick on the *The Wealthy Barber* for a minute, simply because the book was so successful and many Canadians have either heard of it or read it. This book has helped contribute to the investor/saver confusion because of its unrealistic yearly investment return expectation of 15 percent. Since the 1980s, the trend in so-called financial advice has been to sell the dream of earning money without saving. Younger demographics are particularly vulnerable to edgy, high-return investments, often to their long-term detriment. What has developed in the psyche of many people is an unrealistic faith and expectation that through investment returns and the "magic of compound interest" we can accomplish our goals and dreams. We all want our money to work smarter and harder for us, yet for the magic of compound interest to work, you must first establish an ample base amount of financial resources. The problem with placing blind faith in compound interest and investment returns is that we do not take the time to understand the rules or guidelines of investing. Expecting to make money for doing nothing, many people ignore the reality that accumulating wealth takes discipline, sacrifice, and patience, three principles that cannot be accomplished when we do not do our part and save!

Economists and other industry "experts" claim there is no need to worry about the alarming decline in national saving rates in both Canada and the United States because gains in investment and real estate returns compensate for the shortfall in savings. Unfortunately, this myth has gone unchallenged and is patently untrue. Yes, some people have made significant gains in both the stock market and in real estate, but others have lost. Numerous studies have shown that investors do significantly poorer than the mutual funds they are invested in. A study in 2001 showed that over a 20-year period, the average equity investor realized nearly 11 percent less than the stock market. (1) It is not that the stock market or investment funds are performing poorly but rather that over a very short period of time we have been transformed from a nation of great savers into a collective that believes that they are ready to become "investors" without knowing the rules of the game in the investment world.

As a side note, I believe that another reason for poor investment returns is the introduction to online investment statements. Although I do not believe that we must restrict access to account balances, it is important to note that in the information age that we now live in, many of us are more susceptible to making rash and impulsive investment decisions based on short-term information and our fears that are driven by the media. It is important that in regards to your long-term investments, you chart a course for the next five to ten years with your advisor and only review semi-annual and annual statements when they come in the mail. Checking your long-term investments daily or on a weekly basis because of short-term information and panic has proven to be the wrong way to build wealth.

Yet the reality is that regardless of our recognition of the merits of a savings-based strategy, we are bombarded with "professional advice" that is telling us that investment or real estate returns make up or compensate for the savings shortfall. The popular rise of mutual funds in the 1980s and a record bull market in the 1990s fostered an appetite for investment returns. During this period, many people began taking on more risks in their portfolios in an attempt to achieve greater investment returns to compensate for a lack of savings. This has resulted in individuals approaching investing in portfolios with greater risk levels than what many they might truly be comfortable with. The lack of pure saving has created a dangerous desire for higher investment returns to fill the savings gap.

Long-term financial success depends on an annual accumulation of money. This annual accumulation of assets can come from one of two places: savings from income or return on investments. Many of us like to believe that investment returns drive our wealth accumulation; however, the reality is that for the majority of our lives, it is actually our daily saving habits that do the work. Until one's financial base of accumulated savings has exceeded one's annual income, investments alone can never make up the entirety of our financial strategy. For example, let's say that you earn $75,000 per year and have $20,000 in retirement savings. Saving 10 percent of your income into your RRSPs will add $7,500 per year. If your RRSP portfolio earns 8 percent, your account will increase by $1,600 per year, a relatively small amount compared to the $7,500 you can control. It is only when your investment account exceeds your income that the rate of return overtakes saving habits as the primary driver of wealth accumulation. It is at this point when your total investment value exceeds your income that you graduate from being a saver to an investor.

Larger amounts of savings also allow you to adhere to basic investment principles, making you more likely to become a good investor. Savings facilitate "buy low, sell high," "stay invested for the long-term," and take advantage of "dollar-cost averaging." By breaking these principles, you will ultimately get lower returns and less overall wealth. Peter Lynch, a renowned mutual fund manager, lists "patience"—riding out market fluctuations—as a key quality of a successful investor. Given that Canadians are three times more likely to withdraw from their RRSPs than to contribute to them, patience poses an obvious challenge. In fact, one of the biggest mistakes young or new investors make is withdrawing or cashing out their investments for other needs such as debt repayment or other spending. Often this "other spending" is time sensitive and is required immediately. The problem or risk is that when you initially set up your "long-term account" you fall into a more "aggressive long-term" portfolio which experiences larger ups and downs, resulting in timing risk. If you need the money right away and the investments have just dropped, this is the worst time to be selling. If you had adequate savings outside of your RRSP, you would not have to access your RRSP and would give your long-term savings the patience required when it comes to investing.

While it remains important to have your money managed wisely, the primary concern is to build a savings account so that its value equals your income. It is interesting to note that the greatest savers—the Great Depression generation—accumulated vast amounts of wealth largely through guaranteed investment certificates (GIC), with little help from investment professionals. I am not advocating a GIC strategy but want to instead highlight the need to develop a strong willingness to simply just save. The transformation in mentality from a saver to an investor has led to a lack of discipline in saving habits, financial frustration, disappointment, and hardship for many. A mindset of frugality and thrift, rather than seeking investment returns, forms the foundation upon which financial control and independence are built. Financial well-being and success are rooted in a savings-based ideology which is vital in mastering sound finances and successful investment portfolios. Individuals can avoid financial disappointment by focusing on accumulating a savings nest egg. Let others waste their time and energy chasing returns, repeating investment mistakes, and cursing the stock market. Remember that in order to become a brilliant investor you must first be a committed saver.

Increase Your Wealth

In the previous chapter, we explored how embracing constraints in our lives can help us reduce and eliminate debt. We will now explore how a disciplined approach to embracing some constraints may also serve to increase our investment returns. Warren Buffet, one of the world's greatest investors, regularly refers to discipline as an essential tool to becoming a smart investor. Those who are able to practice financial discipline and embrace constraints in their lives have greater freedom and greater success in achieving their financial values and goals.

Many believe that embracing voluntary constraints in our lives limits our freedom of choice and contradicts the notion of being independent. While we are made to believe that we live in a world of choice, the reality is that through our "freedom to choose" we often develop habits that can turn into addictions. When we become addicted, we are no longer able to exert any choice over our decisions and have essentially given up our freedom. From a financial perspective, unlimited choices have led many people to chase investment returns and search for the next "best" investment fund. There are thousands of investment funds in today's mutual fund world. This makes it extremely difficult and overwhelming for people (as well as advisors) to build the "best" investment portfolios. It is important to note that the term *best* is in itself a subjective term. Are we referring to the best absolute returns, best relative returns, best risk adjusted returns, or best returns over a one-, five-, ten-, or twenty-year period? Searching for the best creates an environment where we are always doubting or second guessing our decisions, as there is always a better option out there.

One could convincingly argue that 90 percent of the performance of our investment portfolio is determined by having the correct asset allocation strategy. Given this reality, spending energy and effort on trying to find the best fund will commonly result in a poorer performance. There will always be investments in any given year that will do better than yours. Hindsight is always 20/20 and therefore we must not look to short-term absolute returns as the focus of our financial plan. Rather, your plan should be focused on ensuring appropriate risk levels, saving rates, risk-adjusted returns, and long-term trends. I would argue that the expectation of your investment return should be to achieve a rate of return that is adequate and good enough to meet the objectives of your plan. This expectation, of course, first necessitates the existence of an actual plan. Ask yourself this question: What rate of return does my portfolio need in order for me to retire according to my planned timeline? Your next step is to then seek advice to build a portfolio to help you achieve this target return. For those who are saving 20–30 percent of their gross income, that return is much lower than you might expect. Asset allocation is a broad topic and beyond the scope of this book. For further information, talk to an investment professional about the benefits and importance of asset allocation.

The need to tread our own financial path is crucial in determining the fate of our financial well-being. According to Professor Barry Schwartz, author of *The Paradox of Choice*, we would be much better off financially if we paid less attention to what others were doing.

However, the reality is that the psychology of investing pressures us into following what others are doing so that we do not miss out or get left behind. In his book *Markets, Mobs and Mayhem*, Robert Menschel, Senior Director of the Goldman Sachs Group, discusses the history and psychology of investing, exploring how following the crowd can lead to poor investment decisions and lower returns. It is clearly very important that you understand your own investment philosophy and that you stick to it. Sticking to your own strategy is often the most difficult part of financial planning, especially investing, since doubt often creeps into our mind when we see others behaving in a way that contradicts our plan. This problem is compounded by today's information age in which we are bombarded with conflicting information and opinions that tempt us to abandon our long-term plans because of short-term news. This is where discipline and embracing constraints play a critical role in protecting us from becoming emotionally involved in the investment or saving strategy.

People have varying expectations surrounding their financial plan, the most dangerous being that investment returns should make up any deficiencies in savings. Lowering our expectations about the results of our decisions can significantly improve our financial well-being. An important place to start might be by lowering your expectations regarding your rate of return. An appropriate and anticipated rate of return varies depending on your risk level, time horizon, income bracket, investment knowledge and experience, and financial commitment. Our expectations are clearly out of sync with reality. According to Schwartz, "The amount of choice and control we have, or perceive to have, over most aspects of our lives contributes to high expectations." (2) A perfect example is the expectations that we have regarding investment returns. It is an illusion that we have ultimate control over investment returns. While along with our advisors we may have some influence, to suggest that we have control is misleading and a source of frustration. There are too many factors that are outside of our control, such as interest rate changes, currency fluctuations, local political issues, global political and business challenges, and environmental concerns, to name but a few.

As a very general overview, there are five categories that investors/savers usually fall into: aggressive, advanced, balanced, moderate, or conservative. The difference between these categories is primarily the percent allocation of four asset classes: equities (stocks), fixed income (bonds), cash, and foreign investments. Below are suggested rates of return to use for long-term planning depending on which risk level category you fall into. Putting investment projections in writing is always dangerous, as investment environments constantly change. These numbers may be used as a guideline, but please consult a certified financial planner. The rates below are conservative rates in order to prevent you from falling into the trap of depending on investment returns to achieve your financial goals. I have yet to meet anyone who has said that they have saved too much, but have met many who said that they wished that they had saved more or started earlier. Planning for a 15 percent rate of return and getting 10 percent will mean working many years past your intended retirement. Alternatively, if you plan on 7 percent and get 10 percent, you may be able to retire a couple of years earlier. It is important to note that different companies will have different names for the five categories below and some will have slightly different breakdowns between equities and fixed income, but this is a good starting point.

Aggressive 8–9%   **(100% Equities) (highest % of foreign content)**
Advanced 7–8%   **(80% Equities – 20% Fixed Income)**
Balanced 5–7%   **(60% Equities – 40% Fixed Income)**
Moderate 4–5%   **(40% Equities – 60% Fixed Income)**
Conservative 3–4%   **(25% Equities – 75% Fixed Income)**
                               (lowest % of foreign content)

No category is better than the others. Both the conservative and aggressive saver can achieve early retirement; it is only that the conservative saver will have to save more to make up the difference in the rate of return. Speak with an investment professional to gain a better understanding of where you fit and for a more detailed look at the make-up of each category. Alternatively, you can go to *www.moneyassassins.com* and fill out the investment questionnaire to help you identify your risk profile.

Barry Schwartz believes that we would be better off if our decisions were non-reversible, which scares a lot of people. In all honestly, I must admit that at first it scared me as well. Yet when you sit back and look, you realize that when people are unable to back out of a decision, they tend to make the best of the situation and often reap significant long-term benefits without regret. Defined pension plans are a great example. The employee has no choice in the matter and has to contribute regularly and makes no investment decisions. In the end, when they retire, almost all are happy to have a regular income guaranteed for life. Non-reversible financial products force us to stick to our plan and achieve our goals. Although this may cause some short-term inconveniences, over the long-term we tend to be happy with the end result: more money! Financial planning requires a long-term perspective and too many financial products today allow us to deviate or back out from the intended goal. It is important that you not confuse non-reversible with inflexible. Flexibility is essential to a successful financial plan. While many unpredictable things can happen over the course of your life, if your financial plan is built correctly you should rarely ever have to completely abandon or collapse your plan. With all of this said, I would strongly encourage you to try and find a certified financial planner (CFP) who will take the time to get to know your needs, will explain the finer points of investing, set realistic benchmarks, assess an appropriate risk tolerance and asset allocation program, and who will strongly support the need to get you to save so that there is no confusion when it is time to retire or achieve your goals.

Financial Protection and the World of Personal Insurance

For most people, the weakest part of their financial plan is their failure to adequately protect themselves. The protection aspect of a financial plan is designed to ensure that your current standard of living and financial goals, such as early retirement, are maintained in the event that an illness, injury, or death jeopardizes or alters the individual or family's income. No one likes to think about the possibility of these uncontrollable events, and as a result, we often procrastinate and even avoid the topic altogether. Many people can be heard saying,

"I don't believe in insurance" or "I have enough coverage" or "it's too expensive." Many people feel as though they already have a lot of insurance, as the reality is that we do tend to insure many of our assets, such as our home, vehicle, and appliances. While we often go to great lengths to ensure that our precious assets are insured, we often forget (or neglect) to pay attention to our most valuable asset: ourselves! It should never be forgotten that our greatest financial asset is our ability to earn an income. As many are living on the edge of financial hardship, it is much easier to believe that insurance is useless instead of adopting changes in our lifestyle that will enable us to find the money to pay for the required premiums. While personal insurance may seem costly to some, the truth is that the cost only appears high because we have likely not allocated enough to our financial plan to protection in the first place. For example, if your monthly financial commitment for savings is only $200, an additional $100 per month for insurance seems costly. Yet as we saw earlier in the Heart Attack Graph, you should be committing between 20–30 percent of your income to your financial plan. Once you have committed the recommended savings amount, you will see that premiums are very manageable and economical.

While personal insurance is designed to protect our loved ones, it also serves to protect our own financial dignity. Much of the financial pain and suffering that occurs from sickness, injury, and death is masked due to our increased access to debt and the reality that our net worth statements are not visible to outsiders, friends, family, and colleagues who are obviously blind to the true financial costs of these hardships. The most solid wealth accumulation plan can be completely wiped out by a motor vehicle accident, stroke, cancer, or death. I strongly recommend that all readers complete a thorough insurance/protection review of their financial plan.

There are thousands of mixed messages and opinions about insurance, leaving many with inaccurate information about the pros and cons of all the variety of types of personal insurance. Just like the accumulation aspect of your financial plan should be tailored to fit your personal circumstances, so too should your insurance plan be customized to fit your needs. For our purposes, we will focus on three types of personal insurance that most if not all should consider. We will look at life, critical illness, and disability insurance. Another type of personal insurance, which can play a valuable role in your financial plan is called long-term care. It is designed specifically for individuals who are closing in on retirement and are specifically concerned about the costs of a long-term care facility or home care assistance when they reach their 60s, 70s, 80s, and 90s. Of course, like any other type of personal insurance, the earlier you purchase it the lower the premium, but at younger ages, other types of insurance coverage, like critical illness, seem to be more economical. So for this reason, I have limited discussion of long-term care but would suggest anyone interested in more information to contact a licensed insurance professional. As the world of personal insurance can be complex, it is my goal to give a brief and general overview. For more information about any type of personal insurance, seek an insurance professional or certified financial planner.

Life Insurance

The most important thing to remember when buying life insurance is to ensure that you buy the right *amount* of coverage. Make sure that you avoid getting hung up on trying to buy the best *type* of coverage. Beneficiaries never ask, "What type of life insurance did my spouse have?" Instead, they always ask, "Are we going to be okay? Do we have enough money?" Make sure your advisor completes a full life insurance needs analysis before you purchase any life insurance coverage. Three types of life insurance are available for us to purchase: permanent, temporary, and group coverage. While our needs and reasons for life insurance will change over the course of our lives, the importance of having good coverage should be part and parcel of your financial plan. In the early stages of your coverage, your life insurance will serve to protect family income and cover large debts such as a mortgage. During the years before your retirement, you may use life insurance as a tax shelter to enhance your retirement. During your "golden years," your life insurance becomes an excellent tool of estate planning. For simplicity's sake, and given that the majority of readers fall into the first category, we will focus on the role that life insurance plays in the early stages of your coverage.

During the years of juggling a mortgage and a young family, it is crucial that you have life insurance to protect your family income and pay off debts. Debts that are common at this stage of life include student loans and mortgages. The most economical and practical kind of insurance at this stage of your life is term insurance. Term insurance is designed to give you larger amounts of coverage for very reasonable premiums, but the rates will increase over the course of the policy. The most common term period is ten years, although there are also terms of twenty, five, and one year. This means that if you purchase a ten-year term policy, the rates will be guaranteed for the first ten years and will then increase every ten years thereafter.

It is very important that you recognize that the point of insurance is not to get rich or to make a financial profit from the death of a loved one, but rather to protect the family's current lifestyle and dignity. The appropriate amount of life insurance coverage that you should have is determined by the combination of two components. The first component is the lump sum capital that is required at death to meet immediate needs for cash. Initial lump sum needs can include cash for the elimination of your debts (including your mortgage[s], line of credit and credit cards, payment of burial expenses, tax liabilities and other administrative expenses that may be incurred). Other needs may include a lump sum for education savings for your children, cash on hand for special bequests, and a host of other personal wishes.

The second component is the lump sum capital required to provide an annual income. Calculating this lump sum need is a little more intricate and is more art than science. A number of factors and assumptions contribute to the total amount of your coverage. Some of the main factors include the number of years for the required level of annual income, tax rates, inflation rate, and rates of return on the insurance proceeds. When you are planning for life insurance, it is wise to use more conservative rates given the financial severity that an unexpected death can have on your family's finances. An insurance professional will be able to help you assess your personal needs or you may also visit *www.moneyassassins.com* and fill out the insurance needs analysis.

For most young families, their needs analysis will reveal a need for half a million to a million dollars of coverage. This number tends to scare a lot people, as a million dollars sounds like a lot of coverage, especially if you have not yet saved more than $100,000. The questions that need to be asked though are: What does a million dollars of coverage mean for your family? What type of lifestyle would my family have? For today's average young family, a million dollar policy would roughly eliminate most debts (including your mortgage), provide some funds for a child's education, and provide the family with an annual $50,000 (after-tax) income to live on for 15 years. At the time of writing, a million-dollar, ten-year term policy for a 30-year-old, non-smoking male is approximately $55 a month for the first ten years of the policy. A thirty-year-old, non-smoking female would pay $37 a month for the first ten years of the policy. Therefore, for about $90 a month, a young family is able to have financial security in the event of an unexpected tragic death of a spouse. The financial strain and hardship of not having the coverage is a risk that I am certainly not willing to advise individuals to take.

While we have focused on term insurance up to now, the reality is that a permanent life insurance policy, in conjunction with term insurance, should be a cornerstone of any sound financial strategy. There are two types of permanent life insurance: universal life (UL) and participating (Par) or whole life insurance. Both UL and Par will meet your life insurance needs; the only difference is that they take different paths to get the job done. Permanent life insurance differs from term insurance in a variety of ways, but I will only highlight two. Permanent life insurance has a guaranteed level of cost for insurance while term insurance increases in cost. Permanent life insurance also allows for savings and cash value while term insurance does not.

To fully understand the differences between universal life and whole life insurance requires both time and effort. Yet as a general rule, universal life is more appropriate for the individual who wants more flexibility—a hands-on approach with more options. Participating coverage, on the other hand, is more suitable for the "hands off and lock it in a safe" type of client, with a more fixed-income focus for the cash value. Universal life has gained popularity with advisors over the last few years largely because of changes in the insurance and financial services industry. This, however, should not be interpreted as a sign that it is a superior product to other types of life insurance, as the two are simply different. When you consider a permanent life insurance plan, make sure that your advisor takes into consideration your personality and finance styles.

As I have stressed throughout the course of the book, the key to financial success is to develop a financial plan early on. The same strategy applies regarding your insurance plan. It is important to realize that personal insurance is not a right and is based on your health. When you begin your insurance plan at an earlier stage of your life, you are guaranteed better rates and have a greater potential for larger cash values. To ensure that you have the right type and amount of coverage, I strongly encourage you to seek a financial planning professional who offers term, whole life, and universal life insurance so you can be informed of all your options.

Disability and Critical Illness Insurance

If you owned a black box in the basement of your home that printed $50,000 to $100,000 per year, you would surely want to spend a couple thousand dollars a year to protect it against theft, fire, water, and other damages. Why would you not do the same with yourself, when you consider that your earning potential may be that of the black box? Your ability to earn an income is one of the most valuable financial assets you have, yet so many people forget to protect and insure it. We can all name friends, family, or associates who have lost time from work because of an injury or illness, yet we continue to believe that "it won't happen to me." About one in three people will suffer from a disability or critical illness over the course of their lives. The financial consequences of this suffering can be broad and potentially severe. What makes this even more difficult to accept is that these events are largely out of our control. Seven-time Tour de France winner Lance Armstrong can attest to the reality that even when we are in top physical condition we can be vulnerable to anything. (Lance Armstrong developed testicular cancer in 1996.) Disability and critical illness insurance are complex products with many options that necessitate special attention and explanation. While the complexity of this type of insurance goes beyond the scope of this book, it plays an important role in building a rock solid financial foundation and is a worthy topic to warrant a brief discussion.

The difference between critical illness and disability coverage is demonstrated by the following analogy using the safety features of a vehicle. Think of disability coverage as the brakes on your vehicle and critical illness as the air bag. Just like you would never drive a vehicle without brakes, so too should you never go without disability protection in your financial plan. Most individuals have disability coverage through their employee benefit program at work. Typically, 60 to 70 percent of your income is insured in these programs, but it is always best to inquire into the details of your own plan. For those who are self-employed or have no coverage at work, you must apply for a personal policy through an insurance carrier. While critical illness insurance is nice to have, and in some circumstances should always be included in your plan, it should always be second to a solid disability plan. There was a time when people usually died from heart attacks, strokes, and cancer, yet today many survive and even thrive after such illnesses. However, to fully recover, it is important for individuals to take the time and get the support and care that they need. Surviving such illnesses has meant financial strain and difficulty for many. Furthermore, often the financial strain that is felt by the person who is sick and unable to work is also felt by the caregiver, be it a spouse, friend, child, or other family member, who often jeopardize their income to care for a loved one. As many people are surviving their illnesses and living much longer lives, the only option for many is to use retirement savings, endangering their financial goals such as retirement or an education fund for their children. Critical illness also differs from disability coverage in the way that the benefit is paid out. Disability pays a monthly benefit, while critical illness disperses tax-free lump sum benefits. These lump sum benefits can be used for anything such as income support, a recovery holiday, and additional medical expenses, to name but a few options. Understanding both disability and critical illness coverage is an important part of a well-built financial plan. As I have mentioned throughout the book, in order to have financial control over our lives, we must have options and easy access to financial resources. Disability and critical illness ensure that financial dignity and options are preserved during a time of significant stress. As this coverage plays a vital role in the success of your financial plan, I would encourage you to speak to a licensed insurance professional to help you gain a better understanding of how you might fit this coverage into your plan.

First Steps

We would all agree that an apple is good for our health, but if we tried to eat it in one bite we may choke and probably hurt ourselves trying. But if we take small bites, the apple will be good for us. Our financial plan is no different. Trying to tackle all aspects of financial planning in one bite is difficult and daunting. Begin with small bites and you will eventually take care of it all. We have discussed committing 20–30 percent of your income to your financial plan, we explored the importance of focusing on saving, and we discussed the importance of protecting and insuring yourself, but what is your first bite? Here are the first four steps I would suggest you accomplish to get you started on the right financial path:

1) Begin with calculating your financial ratios: your total debt service ratio, vehicle-to-income ratio, and your income-to-financial plan ratio (Heart Attack Graph). You can calculate all three at the *Money Assassins* website. *www.moneyassassins.com*

2) Invest the time to properly complete the life intentions exercise in Chapter Seven "The Joy of Living Debt Free."

3) Gather all of your current financial documents (savings, investments, insurance, taxes, etc.) and put them in a folder or shoebox— it does not matter what they are in, just have them in one place.

4) Seek professional advice from a certified financial planner who will take the time to invest in you. Your advisor should complete a discovery or fact-finding meeting before they give you any recommendations. To ensure the best comprehensive advice use a financial planner who can offer you both insurance and savings advice and products. In Canada, one way you can locate a certified financial planner is by visiting the Financial Planners Standards Council website at

www.fpsccanada.org and clicking on "Find a Planner." It is important to note that not all certified financial planners are listed, but you can check if the planner you are considering using or currently using is in good standing. In the United States, a planning professional can be found at *www.cfp.net*.

It is empowering to learn that financial wisdom, success, and security are in our hands. It is our personal thoughts, behaviours, and habits that are the building blocks of a strong financial foundation, not rates of returns, interest rates, and other factors beyond our control. Committing 20–30 percent of your income to your financial future is essential, being a great saver leads to brilliant investing, protecting yourself and your family is non-negotiable, and financial planners are one of the few industries on your side in the battle against the Money Assassins.

Over the course of these pages, we have covered a lot ground by examining our history, finding happiness, our children, the social pressures to spend, living "car-lite," buying a home, eliminating debt, and creating wealth. But as we will see in the concluding chapter, courage is the rarest of qualities yet the most powerful and necessary for a financial turnaround! I congratulate you on making this bravest of commitments!

Chapter 9

Summaries

Too much and for too long, we seem to have surrendered personal excellence and community value in the mere accumulation of material things. Our gross national product...if we judge the United States of America by that...counts air pollution and cigarette advertising, and ambulances to clear our highways of carnage. It counts special locks for our doors and the jails for the people who break them. It counts the destruction of the redwoods and the loss of our natural wonder, in chaotic sprawl. It counts napalm and it counts nuclear warheads, and armored cars for police to fight the riots in our cities. It counts Whitman's rifle and Speck's knife, and the television programs which glorify violence in order to sell toys to our children. Yet the gross national product does not allow for the health of our children, the quality of their education, or the joy of their play. It does not include the beauty of our poetry or the strength of our marriages; the intelligence of our public debate or the integrity of our public officials. It measures neither our wit nor our courage; neither our wisdom nor our learning; neither our compassion nor our devotion to our country; it measures everything, in short, except that which makes life worthwhile.
—Speech by Robert Kennedy, March 18th, 1968, University of Kansas.

Weeks before his assassination in 1968, Robert Kennedy gave hope to those who saw a need to change how we view and measure economic progress. But it was his courage to give the speech, in which he challenged the status quo, which is of most importance. Hope has been said to be the foundational quality that inspires change, but hope is the easy part; it is finding the courage to act on ideas and inspiration that tends to be the challenge. Courage is not only required during crucial decisions in our lives but also in our small daily decisions which lay the foundation for us to act with freedom and responsibility. Courage can be scary because it means letting go of the secure and familiar, it demands that we be truthful to our values, ideals, and dreams. It is our fear of being isolated, rejected, or ridiculed that suppresses our courage to be ourselves. (1) But failing to be courageous means a life of conformity and from a financial perspective means a life of debt and financial dejection. Eliminating debt and creating wealth requires the most courageous of tasks—being true to one's self.

Many have a vested interest in undermining our financial courage. Consumer society has influenced us to purchase goods and services, that we do not need nor derive true value from. Our increasing access to debt has fuelled our ability to spend beyond our means, tempted our inner vanity, and has put us in financial harm's way. Technological advances, including debit cards and credit cards, have desensitized us from our relationship with money, encouraging poor financial decisions, and excessive spending. The interplay and influence that the three Money Assassins have on our financial lives have given us valuable insight in answering the question we began with: Why do we spend more than we make? Throughout the book, we have been creating an awareness of the Money Assassins and their role on our social, economic, and private lives. This awareness is fundamental for us to take the first steps in reclaiming our financial control and well-being.

The Great Forgetting

We started our journey to eliminate debt and create wealth by first discovering pearls of wisdom and sage advice from generations past. History has taught us to prepare for economic hardship, to have financial empathy for one another, and to demand greater financial leadership from our governmental officials. Having a new-found appreciation for how survivors of the Depression had to rebuild their financial belief system now gives us permission today to proudly proclaim thrift and frugality as honourable virtues to attain in hopes of reclaiming the lost art of saving.

THREE TAKE-AWAY POINTS:
- **Hard times can hit anyone and come suddenly.**
- **We must encourage government to play a more positive role in fostering a culture of saving.**
- **Financial empathy is crucial to rebuilding our financial belief structure.**

Wealth, Happiness, and the First Assassin

The Japanese have an interesting saying, "The Gods only laugh when people ask them for money." (2) It was in Chapter Two that we saw numerous studies reveal that more money does not mean greater happiness, that pursuing the "perception of wealth" leads to more debt and financial anxiety, and that we already possess many of the riches that we desire. We learned to be aware of relative competition with our peers and consumptive communities and that we must be cautious of our willingness to spend large sums of money to maintain our relative status. In the context of how we measure economic success, Albert Einstein once said, "Try not to become a man of success, but rather try to become a man of value." If, as a society, we continue to use narrowly defined measures of success, such as gross domestic product (GDP), we risk becoming a society of "success" rather than value. We touched on the concept of "financial waste," which simply is the idea of squandering valuable energy and resources simply for the display of wealth and status. It is a new concept that is not fully understood but is nevertheless critical if one strives to have an environmentally sensitive financial plan.

THREE TAKE-AWAY POINTS:
- **More money does not equal greater happiness.**
- **Beware of relativism.**
- **An understanding that Veblen's concept of "waste" is crucial to environment change and action.**

Some readers may have found it surprising to learn that technology was one of the Money Assassins, but after seeing how technology has done more financial harm than good in helping individuals achieve a high level of financial maturity, it is obvious why it warrants being one of the assassins. We saw that technology's greatest influence was in regard to our payment methods and marketers' ability to data-mine and collect information on consumer habits and preferences. To alert and awaken our financial conscience to these attacks we must use more cash, protect our personal information, and question technology and its impact on our personal finances.

THREE TAKE-AWAY POINTS:
- **Pay with cash!**
- **Be aware of how your personal information and preferences are being tracked.**
- **Impulse purchases are the true cost of using debit cards and credit cards, not the fees.**

Groomed to Consume

In a chapter that is shocking to be found in a financial planning book, we learned that family budgets and the financial minds of our children have been under a new type of financial assault since the 1980s. With children influencing, directly and indirectly, hundreds of billions of dollars of spending a year, companies have been racing to brand, capture, and own the consumption preferences of children from the day they are born. This has resulted in children being raised in an economic environment that prioritizes consumption over financial prudence, personal health, and the well-being of our families. We discussed the importance and need to begin to protect the minds of children from a marketing and advertising industry that blatantly endorses the exploitation of children's fears and anxieties. Hundreds if not thousands of dollars a year are stolen from the family coffers as a result of marketing and advertising tactics and it is up to individuals and families, society as a whole, to stand up and say that this is not acceptable and that our children are not for sale.

THREE TAKE-AWAY POINTS:
- Children influence a significant amount of family spending.
- Marketers are aggressively attempting to brand, capture, and own our children.
- Developing a healthy financial belief structure means embracing an alternative to our consumption based lifestyle.

Spending to Belong and the New Necessities: The Second Assassin

At the end of part one, we explored the enormous social pressure to spend to belong. While its presence has gone largely undetected, millions of individuals live with the subconscious fear of being socially excluded if they do not participate in our consumer culture. Marketing and advertising have transformed our relationship with products, and more advanced consumer research has given marketers unprecedented access to the most intimate and personal aspects of our lives. We have seen how marketers have used this new-found information to enhance the effectiveness of product campaigns, by using covert, deceptive, and secretive messaging to exploit our personal insecurities and inadequacies. The result has been the display of an endless array of "new necessities" for us to buy to fill our perceived shortcomings, resulting in an increased baseline of consumption which has pushed many over the edge of financial solvency. Curbing and being aware of our need to "spend to belong" and questioning what our true needs are is essential to a life of financial peace and comfort.

THREE TAKE-AWAY POINTS:
- Be alert to your "consumptive communities" behaviours.
- Do not underestimate the social pressure to consume.
- Rethink want vs. need.

Living "Car-lite"

Habits are hard to break, especially convenient ones (or at least ones that we believe to be convenient). The automotive industry spends millions, if not billions, of dollars annually to ensure that society believes in the dream of private transportation. As we calculated, vehicles, on average, cost individuals 20 percent of their income and life energy. Working one day a week for the privilege of having a vehicle sit idle for the vast majority of the day is an extremely inefficient use of personal wealth. We learned that by implementing the idea of location efficiency and designing our lives around alternative methods and forms of transportation, we can realize significant savings and in the process stumble upon an abundance of free money. Being aware of and calculating one's vehicle expenses is the first step in welcoming a "car-lite" lifestyle. This is one of the simplest, yet admittedly not the easiest, steps in eliminating debt and creating wealth.

THREE TAKE-AWAY POINTS:
- **Calculate all the costs of vehicle ownership and keep your costs below 10 percent of your gross income.**
- **Embrace alternative forms of transportation.**
- **Implement location efficiency into your life.**

Home Cent$

At one time or another, we all have heard the adage "never buy the biggest house on the block," but after our discussion in "Home Cent$," I hope future generations will hear "don't have the largest total debt service ratio on the block." We discussed how home expectations have changed over the years and how we need to re-evaluate housing expectations and truly understand the financial and lifestyle costs of exceeding prudent financial guidelines. We learned to attempt to have a mortgage that is no more than 2.5 times one's household income, to limit the amortization period to a maximum of 25 years, and to beware of using the Home Buyers' Plan as a way to save for a down payment. If you are hoping to buy a home in the future, go and speak to a financial professional today and reduce the likelihood of making a brash emotional mistake with one of the most important financial decisions you will make in your lifetime.

THREE TAKE-AWAY POINTS:
- **Ensure that your total debt service ratio (TDSR) does not exceed 25 percent after including your mortgage.**
- **Manage your emotions during the home buying process.**
- **Avoid the Home Buyers' Plan to fund a down payment.**

The Joy of Living Debt Free: Escaping the Third Assassin

Appearances can be deceiving. Financial well-being is invisible, and while some may appear to be enjoying success, we do not know if they have been burdened with debt payments for life. We would all agree that there is more to life than money, but when burdened with debt, it is easy to lose focus and devote time to other important aspects of our lives. Breaking free from the shackles of debt is one of the most difficult tasks because to kill the root of the problem—our perception of money, success, and wealth—we must go through the challenging process of examining our values and beliefs. I hope after discovering your life's intentions that the road to a debt-free life has been brought into focus.

THREE TAKE-AWAY POINTS:
- **Eliminating debt is more of a psychology strategy than financial.**
- **There is no such thing as "good debt" or "bad debt," all that matters is having a healthy total debt service ratio (TDSR).**
- **Have your Life's Intentions around you all the time and review them often.**

Financial Wisdom

At this point in the book, you should have calculated some financial ratios specific for your personal situation. Key figures that we have calculated are the total debt service ratio, what percentage of your income your vehicle is consuming, the percentage of your income that your mortgage is consuming, and, after completing the Heart Attack Graph, you should know the percentage of your income that you are contributing to your financial plan. If you keep score of these four ratios and commit to improving them, you will be well on your way to creating a financial plan and life full of security, flexibility, and wealth.

THREE TAKE-AWAY POINTS:

- **Commit 20–30 percent of your gross income to your comprehensive financial plan.**
- **Know that becoming an astute saver is a prerequisite to evolving into a brilliant investor.**
- **Protect your most important financial asset: *you*! Explore the world of personal insurance.**

Conclusion

Financial Courage

Moral courage is a rarer commodity than bravery in battle or great intelligence. Yet it is the one essential, vital quality for those who seek to change a world which yields most painfully to change.
—Bobby Kennedy

If you have made it to this point in the book, congratulations! You have taken a major step towards recapturing your financial freedom! We have covered a lot of information and done a lot of work, and it can be overwhelming, especially if one does not know where to begin or have personalized help. The problem with many "self-help" books, including many personal finance books, is that they put the sole burden of solving the problem on the individual, emphasizing that you and you alone can make the change and find the answers. It has been forgotten that meaningful change requires regular support and encouragement from a larger community. Reclaiming our individual financial beliefs and convictions requires society as a whole to awaken to this need for support.

I would encourage you to build a personalized financial support network to encourage you to stay on track and reinforce positive changes and gains. Talk to friends, family, and colleagues about establishing a monthly financial discussion group. Topics can vary from daily financial matters including how to reduce transportation expenses and minimizing child raising costs, to more complex topics such as eliminating debt, how to invest, being tax wise, and insurance planning. These discussion groups provide comfort and a safe place to discuss the much feared topic of money. Brilliant ideas will flourish from your discussions, and the group will be an example to others to the possibility of meaningful change. Also, meet with a certified financial planner who, in addition to encouraging you, will be able to take you through the financial planning process and give you specific advice on a variety of financial strategies and products. Please visit the *Money Assassins* website, *www.moneyassassins.com*, for additional support, encouragement, and up-to-date financial advice.

No one would disagree with the statement that Las Vegas is designed for visitors to spend and lose money, even though many of us go with the belief that it will be a free trip after we included our winnings. It's obvious that the odds are stacked against us, with every move and impulse tracked, planned, and monitored by the establishment. Even smart, disciplined, hard-working individuals fall victim to the well-designed spending, gambling, and consuming atmosphere. So why would we believe an economy fuelled by debt and dependent upon consumer spending for its survival be any different? And now that we have become aware of the Money Assassins' influence and have acquired the necessary skills and knowledge to defeat them, there are no excuses. It is now time for action. It is only in action that our financial and personal lives will improve.

We must demand to be taught our financial history; demand financial protection for our children; demand consumer sovereignty; demand that economic progress be measured for our benefit; demand life without debt; demand a life of joy, thrift, and liberty; and demand that our own governments have a vested interest in our financial well-being. This "financial activism" will not be easy but will be necessary if we strive for a healthier personal, societal, and environmental world.

Tony Benn, a former member of the British parliament, said that those who are shackled with debt do not have the freedom of choice and if individuals broke free from those shackles, a "democratic revolution" would occur. (1) My hope is that when financial archeologists dig a hundred years from now they will find remnants of a society that had the courage to bring about a financial, social, and environmental revolution which began with aggressive savings, using cash, eliminating debt, delaying gratification, and living by the words of "waste not, want not." I hope by exposing the Money Assassins, we will find the courage and resolve to act to revive the lost art of saving and take the first steps toward igniting this financial revolution!

A great amount of courage and dignity is required to live within one's means and I would encourage you to share the message of thrift, frugality, and saving with others. It is the action of others that is the greatest persuader and we must be the action and change that others see and admire. There is a great deal of urgency in the need to expose the Money Assassins and their plans. Tell others about the Money Assassins before they ruin more financial lives. Creating wealth and eliminating debt is simple, it is just not always easy. I hope you have found this book to be a valuable resource and a catalyst to a life of financial well-being!

Your Help Is Needed!

Life is about paying it forward and helping others. If you have found this book to be of value, don't keep it a secret. Every day, more and more individuals lose their financial security to the Money Assassins. Time is of the essence. There is a great deal of urgency in making individuals aware of the Money Assassins—you can help them! Tell people in your life about the book, give them a copy, and if you would like to buy a copy for someone you care about, visit our website

www.moneyassassins.com

to find out how to have a signed personalized copy sent to a friend, family member, or colleague.

Thank you for doing your part to help defeat the Money Assassins and revive the lost art of saving!

Best Wishes,
Chad Viminitz

References

Introduction

(1) Schumacher, E.F. 1973. *Small Is Beautiful: Economics As If People Mattered.* New York: Harper & Row.

(2) Korten, D.C. 1995. *When Corporations Rule the World.* West Hartford: Kumarian Press, Inc.

(3) Broadfoot, B. 1973. *Ten Lost Years, 1929-1939: Memories of Canadians Who Survived.* Toronto: McClelland & Stewart.

(4) Schor, J.B. 2004. *Born to Buy: The Commercialized Child and the New Consumer Culture.* New York: Scribner.

(5) Cialdini, R.B. 1993. *Influence: The Psychology of Persuasion.* New York: William Morrow.

(6) Balish, C. 2006. *How to Live Well Without Owning a Car: Save Money, Breathe Easier, and Get More Mileage Out of Life.* Berkeley: Ten Speed Press.

(7) Manning, R.D. 2000. *Credit Card Nation: The Consequences of America's Addiction to Credit.* New York: Basic Books.

Chapter One

(1) Terkel, S. 1970. *Hard Times: An Oral History of the Great Depression.* New York: The New Press.

(2) Quinn, D. 1997. *The Story of B.* New York: Bantam.

(3) Broadfoot, B. 1973. *Ten Lost Years, 1929-1939: Memories of Canadians Who Survived.* Toronto: McClelland & Stewart.

(4) Galbraith, J.K. 1997. *The Great Crash 1929.* 7th ed. Boston: Houghton Mifflin.

(5) Korten, D.C. 1995. *When Corporations Rule the World.* West Hartford: Kumarian Press.

(6) De Graaf, J., D. Wann, and T.H. Naylor. 2001. *Affluenza: The All-Consuming Epidemic.* San Francisco: Berrett-Koehler.

(7) Manning, R.D. 2000. *Credit Card Nation: The Consequences of Amer-*

ica's Addiction to Credit. New York: Basic Books.

(8) Phillips, K. 2002. *Wealth And Democracy: A Political History of the American Rich.* New York: Broadway.

(9) Leiss, W., S. Kline, S. Jhally, J. Botterill. 2005. *Social Communication In Advertising: Consumption in the Mediated Marketplace.* 3rd ed. New York: Routledge Taylor & Francis.

Chapter Two

(1) Adams, M. 2000. *Better Happy Than Rich?: Canadians, Money and the Meaning of Life.* Toronto: Penguin.

(2) Veblen, T. 1998. *The Theory of the Leisure Class.* Amherst: Prometheus.

(3) Anielski, M. 2007. *The Economics of Happiness: Building Genuine Wealth.* Gabriola Island: New Society.

(4) De Graaf, J., D. Wann, and T.H. Naylor. 2001. *Affluenza: The All-Consuming Epidemic.* San Francisco: Berrett-Koehler.

(5) Dominguez, J. and V. Robin. 1992. *Your Money Or Your Life: 9 Steps to Transforming Your Relationship with Money and Achieving Financial Independence.* New York: Penguin.

(6) Frank, R.H. 1999. *Luxury Fever: Money and Happiness in an Era of Excess.* Cambridge: Princeton UP.

(7) Hawken, P. 1993. *The Ecology of Commerce: A Declaration of Sustainability.* New York: HarperBusiness.

(8) Taylor B. 2003. *What Kids Really Want That Money Can't Buy.* New York: Warner.

(9) Korten, D.C. 1995. *When Corporations Rule the World.* West Hartford: Kumarian Press.

(10) Leiss, W., S. Kline, S. Jhally, J. Botterill. 2005. *Social Communication In Advertising: Consumption in the Mediated Marketplace.* 3rd ed. New York: Routledge Taylor & Francis.

(11) Manning, R.D. 2000. *Credit Card Nation: The Consequences of America's Addiction to Credit.* New York: Basic Books. .

(12) Myers, D.G. 1992. *The Pursuit of Happiness: Discovering the Pathway to Fulfillment, Well-Being, and Enduring Personal Joy.* New York: Avon.

(13) Schwartz, B. 2004. *The Paradox of Choice: Why More is Less.* New York: HarperCollins.

(14) Schor, J.B. 2004. *Born to Buy: The Commercialized Child and the New Consumer Culture.* New York: Scribner.

(15) Schor, J.B. 1998. *The Overspent American: Why We Want What We Don't Need.* New York: Basic Books.

(16) Segal, J.M. 1999.*Graceful Simplicity: The Philosophy and Politics of the Alternative American Dream.* 1st ed. New York: Henry Holt & Company.

(17) Wesley, J. "The Use of Money." http://www.ucafunds.com.au/main.php?id=5295. (accessed May 15, 2009).

Chapter Three

(1) Bakan, J. 2004. *The Corporation: The Pathological Pursuit of Profit and Power.* Toronto: Viking Canada.

(2) Linn, S. 2004. *Consuming Kids: Protecting Our Children from the Onslaught of Marketing and Advertising.* New York: The New Press.

(3) Korten, D.C. 1995. *When Corporations Rule the World.* West Hartford: Kumarian Press.

(4) McNeal, J.U. 1992. *Kids as Customers: A Handbook of Marketing to Children.* New York: Lexington.

(5) Schor, J.B. 2004. *Born to Buy: The Commercialized Child and the New Consumer Culture.* New York: Scribner.

(6) Adams, M. 2000. *Better Happy Than Rich?: Canadians, Money and the Meaning of Life.* Toronto: Penguin.

(7) Kilbourne, J. 2000. *Can't Buy My Love: How Advertising Changes the Way We Think and Feel.* New York: Simon and Schuster.

(8) Schlosser, E. 2002. *Fast Food Nation.* New York: Houghton Mifflin.

(9) Taylor B. 2003. *What Kids Really Want That Money Can't Buy.* New York: Warner.

(10) Gardner, H. 2004. *Changing Minds: The Art and Science of Changing Our Own and Other People's Minds.* Boston: Harvard Business School.

Chapter Four

(1) De Graaf, J., D. Wann, and T.H. Naylor. 2001. *Affluenza: The All-Consuming Epidemic.* San Francisco: Berrett-Koehler.

(2) Lindstrom, M. 2008. *Buyology: Truth and Lies About Why We Buy.* 1st ed. New York: Doubleday.

(3) Leiss, W., S. Kline, S. Jhally, J. Botterill. 2005. *Social Communication In Advertising: Consumption in the Mediated Marketplace.* 3rd ed. New York: Routledge Taylor & Francis.

(4) Lindstrom, M. 2008. *Buyology: Truth and Lies About Why We Buy.* 1st ed. New York: Doubleday.

(5) Cialdini, R.B. 1993. *Influence: The Psychology of Persuasion.* New York: William Morrow.

(6) Schor, J.B. 1998. *The Overspent American: Why We Want What We Don't Need.* New York: Basic Books.

(7) Morris, H. 2008. Canadians Uncomfortable Talking about Money. *Financial Post,* August 7.

(8) Betts KD. Positional Goods and Economics. http://home.vic-net.net.au/~aespop/positionalgoods.htm. (Accessed May 1, 2009).

(9) Lasn, K. 1999. *Culture Jam: How to Reverse America's Suicidal Consumer Binge—and Why We Must.* New York: HarperCollins.

(10) Kilbourne, J. 2000. *Can't Buy My Love: How Advertising Changes the Way We Think and Feel.* New York: Simon and Schuster.

(11) Hawken, P. 1993. *The Ecology of Commerce: A Declaration of Sustainability.* New York: HarperBusiness.

(12) Dominguez, J. and V. Robin. 1992. *Your Money or Your Life: 9 Steps to Transforming Your Relationship with Money and Achieving Financial Independence.* New York: Penguin.

(13) Linn, S. 2004. *Consuming Kids: Protecting Our Children from the Onslaught of Marketing and Advertising.* New York: The New Press.

(14) Schwartz, B. 2004. *The Paradox of Choice: Why More is Less.* New York: HarperCollins.

(15) Frank, R.H. 1999. *Luxury Fever: Money and Happiness in an Era of Excess.* Cambridge: Princeton UP.

(16) Underhill, P. 2000. *Why We Buy: The Science of Shopping.* New York, N.Y.: Simon & Schuster.

(17) Klein, N. 2000. *No Logo: Taking Aim at the Brand Bullies.* Toronto: Vintage Canada.

(18) Bakan, J. 2004. *The Corporation: The Pathological Pursuit of Profit and*

Power. Toronto: Viking Canada.

(19) Myers, D.G. 1992. *The Pursuit of Happiness: Discovering the Pathway to Fulfillment, Well-Being, and Enduring Personal Joy.* New York: Avon.

(20) Manning, R.D. 2000. *Credit Card Nation: The Consequences of America's Addiction to Credit.* New York: Basic Books.

(21) Taylor B. 2003. *What Kids Really Want That Money Can't Buy.* New York: Warner.

Chapter Five

(1) Balish, C. 2006. *How to Live Well Without Owning a Car: Save Money, Breathe Easier, and Get More Mileage Out of Life.* Berkeley: Ten Speed Press.

(2) Kilbourne, J. 2000. *Can't Buy My Love: How Advertising Changes the Way We Think and Feel.* New York: Simon and Schuster.

(3) Frank, R.H. 1999. *Luxury Fever: Money and Happiness in an Era of Excess.* Cambridge: Princeton University Press.

(4) Cialdini, R.B. 1993. *Influence: The Psychology of Persuasion.* New York: William Morrow.

(5) TD Canada Trust. How to Choose the Right Vehicle. http://www.tdcanadatrust.com/autoexplorer/cartips3.jsp. (accessed October 9, 2008).

(6) Hawken, P. 1993. *The Ecology of Commerce: A Declaration of Sustainability.* New York: HarperBusiness.

(7) Gilbert, D. 2007. *Stumbling on Happiness.* Toronto: Vintage Canada.

Chapter Six

(1) Advisor.ca. Homebuyers not seeking financial advice: survey. www.advisor.ca/shared/print.jsp?content=20050404_141928_912. (accessed april 6, 2005).

(2) Frank, R.H. 1999. *Luxury Fever.* Cambridge: Princeton UP.

Chapter Seven

(1) Manning, R.D. 2000. *Credit Card Nation: The Consequences of America's Addiction to Credit.* New York: Basic Books.

(2) May, R. 1953. *Man's Search for Himself.* 8th ed. New York: Dell.

(3) Schor, J.B. 1998. *The Overspent American: Why We Want What We*

Don't Need. New York: Basic Books.

(4) Dominguez, J. and V. Robin. 1992. *Your Money Or Your Life: 9 Steps to Transforming Your Relationship with Money and Achieving Financial Independence.* New York: Penguin.

(5) Nemeth, M. 1999. *The Energy of Money: A Spiritual Guide to Financial and Personal Fulfillment.* New York: Ballantine.

(6) Schwartz, B. 2004. *The Paradox of Choice: Why More is Less.* New York: HarperCollins.

(7) Myers, D.G. 1992. *The Pursuit of Happiness: Discovering the Pathway to Fulfillment, Well-Being, and Enduring Personal Joy.* New York: Avon.

(8) De Graaf, J., D. Wann D, and T.H. Naylor. 2001. *Affluenza: The All-Consuming Epidemic.* San Francisco: Berrett-Koehler.

(9) Phillips, K. 2002. *Wealth And Democracy: A Political History of the American Rich.* New York: Broadway.

(10) McFeat, T. Students in Debt. CBC News Online. www.cbc.ca/news/background/personalfinance/studnetdebt.html. (accessed March 16, 2005).

(11) Pachner, J. Student Debt: Coping Strategies for the Scholarly Tab. CBC News Online. Available at: http://www.cbc.ca/news/background/personalfinance/studentdebt2.html. (accessed May 1, 2009).

(12) MuchMusic. MuchMusic Prepaid MasterCard. www.muchmusic.com/muchmusiccard/index.asp. (accessed May 1, 2009).

Chapter Eight

(1) Dalbar Inc. More Proof that Marketing Timing Doesn't Work for the Majority of Investors. www.dalbarinc.com/content/printerfriendly.asp?page=2001062100. (accessed June 21, 2001).

(2) Schwartz, B. 2004. *The Paradox of Choice: Why More is Less.* New York: HarperCollins.

Chapter 9

(1) May, R. 1953. *Man's Search for Himself.* 8th ed. New York: Dell.

(2) Dominguez, J. and V. Robin. 1992. *Your Money Or Your Life: 9 Steps to Transforming Your Relationship with Money and Achieving Financial Independence.* New York: Penguin.

Conclusion

(1) Moore, M. *Sicko*. DVD. Directed by Michael Moore. Denver: Meghan O'Hara, 2007.